Enjoy the
Trip!

Journey to Jesus

Journey to Jesus

Looking for God in All the Right Places

FLORENCE LITTAUER
with
MARITA LITTAUER

HENSLEY
PUBLISHING

Tulsa, Oklahoma

HENSLEY
PUBLISHING

ISBN 1-56322-089-X

Journey to Jesus: Looking for God in All the Right Places

About Photocopying

First Timothy 5:17—18 instructs us to give the laborer his wages, specifically those who labor in the Word and doctrine. Hensley Publishing has a moral, as well as legal, responsibility to see that our authors receive fair compensation for their efforts. Many of them depend upon the income from the sale of their books as their sole livelihood. So, for that matter, do the artists, printers, and numerous other people who work to make these books available to you. Please help us by discouraging those who would copy this material in lieu of purchase.

Contents

SECTION ONE

Preparing for the Journey

My Own Journey to Jesus

Like many of you who are about to begin this Bible study, I spent years looking for God — in all the wrong places. As I was growing up, I had an underlying desire for God. I didn't know what caused that magnetic feeling, but I was drawn to church and involved in all they had to offer. Good works, moral principles, and Bible stories summed up our focus, yet I always knew there had to be something more than activities. When the late R. G. LeTourneau, a wealthy businessman-turned-evangelist, came to our church to hold a series of meetings, I went each evening to hear him. To my recollection, he was the only hint of revival our church ever had, and I listened to every word he had to say.

On the last night he was there, he must have touched my heart with the Word of God, for when he asked for those of us who wanted to work for God and someday go into Christian service to come forward, my eight-year-old brother, Jim, and I walked down the aisle hand in hand. When Mr. LeTourneau asked Jim what he wanted to do for God, he replied that he wished to be a minister when he grew up. The large balding, bespectacled man patted him on the head and then asked me the same question. I replied brightly that I wanted to be a minister too. I had always wanted to be up front. But his answer confused me. "Girls can't be ministers," he said. I was disappointed but was not about to give up: "Then what could I be?" He suggested that I be a missionary. Even though I was only twelve years old, I already knew I didn't have a feel for jungles. Mother had often stated her hope that "they" — I never really learned who "they" were — would never send her to Africa. "They" never did, but by that time she had solidly instilled in me a fear of the mission field. And so I asked again, "What else could I do?" as I stared up at the minister in hopes of an alternative suggestion.

"You get ready, and when you grow up, God will show you His plan," he replied.

I didn't like waiting in suspense, so the next Sunday I asked my Sunday school teacher if a girl could become a minister. She answered quickly, "Good heavens, no! They'd never let us stand up there in a black robe and preach." Apparently she knew the same imposing "they" as my mother did, and I began to accept the fact that "they" would never let me be a minister.

In college at the University of Massachusetts, I went to church faithfully while others slept in on Sunday mornings. I even attended the Protestant student meetings peopled by some of the dullest and least sophisticated coeds on campus. After graduation I returned to my church in Haverhill, got married in it four years later, and then suddenly found that I was expected to go to Fred's "church" — which was one of the major cults in America.

At that time, I didn't know what a cult was, and the fact that this religion put another book on an equal level with the Bible and another person above Jesus didn't deeply concern me. For ten years, Fred and I attended the meetings faithfully every Sunday. We had no idea we were actually wandering around, lost in the wilderness, dying in a spiritual desert.

Within three years, I gave birth to two sons who were both fatally brain-damaged. Practitioners from Fred's church tried to heal them, and when that failed, I was told it was my lack of faith that prevented their cure. If I could only embrace their beliefs and look at my babies as perfect, they would be healed. Once again, I started looking for God. I cried out to the Lord, prayed as the church instructed, and even attended special counseling sessions, but both of the boys died. *If there was a God,* I wondered, *how could problems like these come to such a good person as me?*

Fred and I gave up on the church. We intended to give up on God. We both felt let down by organized religion, ignored by pious pretenders, and depressed by our circumstances. One night Fred came home with an armload of big books on the various religions of the world. He'd been looking for God in the library. "There must be some church that is right for us," he stated as he placed the books on his desk. Every evening he studied and worked on a comparison chart he had made on cardboard of the doctrines and beliefs of different denominations — in the hopes of finding something with which to replace his religion. How I wish we still had that chart, for while we didn't know it at the time, that was the first step in Fred's search for God. Although we'd turned our backs on "church," we both knew there was something missing in our lives besides our sons. We had a "chasm of emptiness" that nothing seemed to fill. Even the chart didn't help; it only categorized choices of churches, none of which seemed to suit our needs. Fred systematized synods and delineated denominations. He created his own special church on the piece of cardboard, returned the texts to the library, and never mentioned the study again. Fred was a deep, thoughtful, analytical, and melancholy person, and once he had placed a perfect God on paper and built a customized church in his own mind, he was through with the project.

One feature Fred had found in his search and had added to his composite religion was a practice in pantheism, in which the Greeks worshiped God among the trees and found spiritual truth in nature. On Sunday mornings, Fred practiced his own version of pantheism: He would put on his white shorts, take his tennis racquets in hand, and head to the country club saying, "You can be just as close to God on the tennis courts as you can in church." The fact that he made an excuse each week showed that he felt guilty, but the statement somehow eased his conscience.

One day Fred's brother, Dick, who had been brought up in the same cult, told us he had been watching a religious program on television, and at the end he and his wife, Ruth, had knelt in front of the television set and asked Jesus to come into their lives. Fred and I had never heard of someone finding God — or even looking for God — on television, but we did see change take place in their lives as we observed them critically over the next year.

When Ruth took me to a Christian Women's Club, I must have been ready, for I began to feel that the speaker, Roy Gustafson, was addressing me personally. Using Romans 12:1–2 as his text, he told us that God wanted us to present our bodies as a living sacrifice. I had no idea what the Bible meant about bringing a sacrifice to the altar, but when he got to the part of not being conformed to the world, I suddenly realized that I had spent my whole life wandering in the wilderness of the world, and for what? The speaker then explained that God would transform our minds if we'd let Him; He would come into our lives and show us what was His good, acceptable, and perfect will for each one of us.

When he told us that we could find God right in that restaurant, I prayed with him as he instructed and asked Jesus into my heart, taking my first baby step toward knowing God. Within a year, Fred and our two daughters, Lauren and Marita, had all dedicated their lives to the Lord. We had been committed Christians for less than two years when we were invited onto the staff of Campus Crusade for Christ. We moved our family from Connecticut to San Bernardino, California. It was there that I began to study God's Word seriously.

Because Bible stories had always been exciting to me, and I knew the people and places so well that I had actually won a district award in my denomination as a pre-teen, I felt as if I had a firm grasp of the Scriptures. When I attended my first Bible study on Genesis, I assumed I would be the star pupil since I could recite the genealogy from Adam to Joseph by heart and I knew the order in which God created the world. Imagine my surprise when, after reading the first verse of the first chapter of Genesis, the teacher showed us that God was plural and that Christ had been with God the Father in creation. By way of explanation, she referred us to the first chapter of John, where we learned that Christ, "the Word," was the beginning. *The Word was with God, and the Word was God. He was with God in the beginning. Through him all things were made; without him nothing was made that has been made* (John 1:1–3).

That passage seemed to clearly point out that Christ and the Father are one and that Jesus had been present and active during the entire creation of the world. It didn't say that He showed up every now and then, but it said that without Him nothing was made. That was a clear statement. I couldn't refute the evidence. Here, while studying the opening verse of the Bible, I discovered that I didn't know what I thought I'd known. I hadn't known that Christ was a part of the Old Testament — I thought He made His first appearance in the manger. Hadn't I recited the Christmas story from Luke in church when I was just three years old? As I was running this question through my head, but not wanting to appear ignorant, another lady voiced my very thoughts: "You mean Jesus was around before He was born?"

Barbara Fain, our teacher, replied that although it didn't make human sense, God was a triune God: Father, Son, and Holy Spirit. We all agreed we'd heard that, but didn't think it happened before the Gospels and Acts. Barbara had us read John 1:10: *He was in the world, and though the world was made through him, the world did not recognize him.*

Our little group was proof of that! Barbara showed us that when He came to earth no one believed that He was God in the flesh, but John 1:14 says, *The Word became flesh and made his dwelling among us. We have seen his glory, the glory of the One and Only, who came from the Father, full of grace and truth."*

We all agreed that it did say that, and then Barbara showed us John 1:12, which told us that if we would believe in Jesus and receive Him into our lives, He would make us children of God — a part of His family.

That day as two others prayed and asked "the Word" to come into their lives and dwell in them, my eyes were opened to my ignorance of the depth and the power of the Scriptures. We hadn't even gotten past the first verse of Genesis, yet we had met the Father, the Son, and the Holy Spirit and had two new believers in the kingdom.

As it turned out, we spent months in that verse-by-verse study of Genesis, and during that time, I became a fervent Bible student. Two years later, when Barbara moved to Atlanta, I was able to step in as the teacher. Since that time, I have spent many years studying and teaching the Bible and helping people in their search for God.

What about you?

Are you like I was, looking for God in all the wrong places? Or have you found Jesus but desire a deeper relationship with Him?

These pages will take you on a journey back to the beginning of time and the creation of the world. They will take you through the ancient stories of the Fall, the Tower of Babel, Abraham, Isaac, Jacob, Joseph, and Moses. But they will also take you on a journey to meet Jesus face to face. And as we walk together through the books of Genesis and Exodus, we will learn more about our Savior than we ever dreamed possible.

> *You will call, and the LORD will answer; you will cry for help and he will say:*
> *"Here am I."*
>
> —Isaiah 58:9

Using This Tour Guide

Before going on any trip, most of us do several things. We often start by talking with friends who have been on a similar journey, in order to check on their adventure, find out what to avoid, what not to miss, and how to pack. When we have confirmed that we are indeed going on this particular trip, we study guidebooks to help us prepare. And then, we pack.

It would be foolish to just jump in the car and go, having no idea what we might encounter or what we would need along the way. That approach would possibly work for a surprise day trip, but not for an extended journey.

As for any trip, you will need to pack. This study — your tour guide manual — is your primary piece of luggage, for you will use it at each and every stop on your journey. But you will also need your Bible because it is your roadmap; it is what this study is all about. If you use two or more different versions of the Bible, pack them all. It will add a deeper dimension to your understanding if you read the same passage from different translations. While each will say the same basic thing, they may use some different word choices that will help to clarify the meaning. Some versions you might want to consider include the *New King James Version* or the *New International Version*. Both of these are very popular, and if you are studying in a group, many people will probably have them. They are very similar to what you may recall from your childhood but without archaic language with words such as "thee" and "thou." A few more modern translations that are widely accepted by scholars and theologians are the *New Century Version* and the *New Living Translation*. Both of these have a style that is more familiar to our ear today, while still staying true to the biblical message. Of course, if you love the classic *King James Version,* it will work as well.

If you do not have a Bible with which you are comfortable, I suggest that you visit a Christian bookstore and spend some time looking through all of the above-mentioned versions — and even some others — to determine which is the best for you. If you are new to studying the Bible, you may want to purchase a Bible with "tabs" that indicate the location of the books of the Bible. These stick out slightly to help you find the different books as you search for the texts cited throughout this study. These tabs can also be purchased separately and attached to your existing Bible.

While you are at the bookstore, you may also want to pick up a basic concordance — available in both book form or software. This will help you find verses in the Bible that are on specific topics. A good study Bible usually has a concordance as a part of the supplemental materials in the back of it. Throughout this study, you will be asked to search for a verse on a specific topic. If you do not have a concordance, you can simply skip this step and, if you are in a group, listen to the verses others select. Write their verses down to look up at home.

When you are ready to take this *Journey to Jesus,* you will find that it is made up of twenty-one stops (lessons) that lead us to our final destination, found in lesson 22 — the goal of our journey. Each stop has some teaching — much like the tour guide who tells you about the location before you are allowed to go out on your own and explore. Within each stop are several items of note. Just like you would do if you were touring a physical site, you will want to stop and consult the map to know where you are. In this study, the sections titled *Consulting the Map* will send you to God's Word, the Bible, to see what He has to say about this particular topic. If you are doing a group study, you will want to do this part at home before you come together so you can share your answers and discuss your insights.

At the end of each lesson you will also find the *Trip Journal.* As you might do on a journey, you will record your thoughts and feelings here. These may be shared with the group as well — or they may be too personal and remain for your eyes only.

Some lessons will also have a section entitled *For Your Notebook.* As might occur on a trip, there will be occasional items of interest of which you will want to make note. For this section, you may want to purchase a small spiral notebook, use a journal, or simply write on the pages at the back of this book.

Traveling on a long trip requires breaks. Here we are calling these *Rest Stops.* The Rest Stops call for quiet times of personal reflection on what you may be learning. In addition, there are several *Scenic Overlooks* along the way — real-life stories that can give you a broader perspective on the topic at hand. Rest Stops and Scenic Overlooks are not included in every lesson, but are interspersed throughout the journey to give you a break from the heavy traveling.

Now let's get started on our *Journey to Jesus!*

Your Own Search for God

"Whenever times get bad, the desire for God gets stronger." These are words I've heard most of my life, but events in the last few years have brought new meaning to this old statement. Terrorism, war, economic woes, and other turmoils have caused a new and intense quest for the sacred in our land. Many people are on a renewed search for God, but so many of them are looking in the wrong places.

WRONG WAY!

Many people's search for God — although sincere — can lead them down a "wrong-way" path to destruction. Below is a short list of ways to look for God in "all the wrong places." Do you know anyone who has ever traveled these paths? Have you ever traveled them yourself?

1. Church

When churches become more like social clubs than the house of God, or when church members behave in ungodly ways, it can drive people farther away from God. Some people "church hop" — going from church to church, not even understanding what they are searching for. God can be found in church — but only when the people in the church point the way to a personal relationship with Jesus.

2. Inspiring Individuals

Dynamic, inspiring pastors and evangelists can point the way *to* God, but they are not gods themselves! Have you ever known anyone who had such a void in their own life that they practically worshiped their pastor or someone else in church leadership? Take care not to mistake God's "man of the hour" for God Himself.

3. Television

Televangelists abound on the airwaves, but is it really possible to find God through a television program? Some people who don't go to church look for

God on TV in the quiet confines of their home — but to many, He seems so expensive. *Does God really cost that much?* they wonder. Salvation is a free gift — no one should ever ask you to pay for it! God can be found on television, but be careful who you watch.

4. Psychological or Psychiatric Therapy

So many people in therapy or under psychiatric care are actually on a search for God. While there is nothing wrong with seeking psychological help for your problems, it alone will never be able to provide you with all of the answers you need.

5. Cults and New Religions

Some people have given up on the church altogether, but in their search for something that transcends their own existence, they have turned to cults or other new religions. The New Age movement is so attractive to many today because it seems to offer spiritual answers and guidance to a population seeking this kind of knowledge. But these will never fully satisfy.

6. Intellectual Pursuits

How many of our impressionable young people, thirsty for knowledge, head off to college — or even seminary — expecting to find the answers to all of the world's problems? Sadly, the true answer is hard to find in the humanistic and relativistic patterns of thought rampant in America's colleges and universities today.

7. Psychic Phenomena

Astrology, channeling, speaking with the dead, reincarnation and dream interpretation remain of primary interest among those who are seeking meaning in life. Unfortunately, not only do these paths *not* lead to God, but they are slippery roads which lead directly downhill.

Where is God today? Is He in the church coffee hour or the Rotary Club? Is He in a pastor or a priest? Is He in money or the media? Is He in cults, in a college classroom, or in "transcendental meditation"? Is He in fortune-tellers, mediums, or psychics? Is God in the cards, in a crystal, or in reincarnation? Never have there been so many diverse groups claiming to have kidnapped God and keeping Him exclusively for their adherents.

If you've been running from place to place in a desperate search for spiritual experiences, I've got good news. God can meet you today, just where you are, right now!

Throughout your own life, where have you looked for God?

_____

_____

Did you find Him in those places?

_____

We are all looking for God to fill that "chasm of emptiness" in our souls, but what we choose to fill that chasm may be less than satisfying. Some choose to fill it with drugs and alcohol, some with sex, others with religion, but that void can only truly be filled with a personal relationship with the Savior, Jesus Christ.

Consulting the Map

Read Acts 17:27.
What does this verse tell us about our search for God?

_____

_____

As we follow the footsteps of history as it is revealed in the books of Genesis and Exodus, we will discover the answer to our search for God — and it ends in a relationship with the Lord Jesus Christ. Whatever religious background we come from, whatever church we attend today, we're all in a search for the sacred, a quest for a personal relationship with God. That relationship can only be found through Christ.

What are some of the places in which people look for God?

_____

_____

Can God be found anywhere?

_____

Do you think that God punishes people for the wrong places they may have looked for Him?

_____

_____

Read Deuteronomy 4:28–31.

According to this passage, what is important in one's search for God?

_____

_____

Read Job 23:3.

Is our generation the only one to struggle to find God?

_____

_____

Read Job 23:4–6.

Why was Job looking for God?

_____

How does Job's quest compare to your own?

_____

_____

Read John 14:6–7.

How do we come to the Father? How do we know what the Father is like?

_____

_____

_____

Let's put on our walking shoes and start looking for God in all the right places, as opposed to the wrong ones. Let's take the first step on our _Journey to Jesus._

It is time to seek the LORD.

—Hosea 10:12

Rest Stop

Have you ever taken the time to ask Jesus Christ to come into your life as your personal Lord and Savior?

_____

If so, spend some time in prayer, thanking Him for what He has done for you. If you have never asked Him into your heart and life, why not do so now? Pray the following prayer:

> *Lord Jesus,*
> *Come into my life. Change me. Make into what You want me to be. I pray this in Your name, amen.*

> *Therefore, I urge you, brothers, in view of God's mercy, to offer your bodies as living sacrifices, holy and pleasing to God — this is your spiritual act of worship. Do not conform any longer to the pattern of this world, but be transformed by the renewing of your mind. Then you will be able to test and approve what God's will is — his good, pleasing and perfect will.*
>
> —Romans 12:1–2

Trip Journal

Think about and then answer the following questions in your journal.

1. As a child, how did you picture God? (For example, a mean old man, a judge, an angel, etc.)

2. Now that you have read God's Word, how is your viewpoint different?

3. Was there ever a time when you gave up on God? What were the circumstances?

4. Did your church help or hurt you at that time? In what ways? Was a feeling of guilt ever put upon you? What did people say about your "lack of faith"?

5. Where did you turn in your search for God? When and where did you find Him? Was there a TV program, a book, or another person that helped you in your search for God?

6. Did anyone try to stop your search?

7. Has your search for God ended? If so, how? If not, in what ways are you still looking?

8. Describe how a search for God must ultimately end in the acceptance of Jesus as Lord and Savior.

Scenic Points of Interest Along the Way

LESSON 2

In the Garden

Read Genesis 1–3.

Every rocket needs a launching pad; each board game, a square-one; each baseball diamond, a home plate; and each journey, a beginning. In the very beginning of time, God created the heavens and the earth. He created day and night; water, land, and sky; plants and trees; seasons, days, and years; sun, moon, and stars; birds, fish, and animals; and man and woman. Our *Journey to Jesus* starts us off in Genesis, "the beginning."

For God's People in Bible Times

In the third verse of Genesis, we see that God, unlike most of us, spoke words before there were any people to hear Him. *And God said, "Let there be light," and there was light* (Genesis 1:3). God spoke; God had power; God could bring about change; God could create. He made trees that were pleasing to the eye and that produced good food. In fact, after He planted this garden in Eden, He even put gold and onyx in the ground to be unearthed. When He created the first couple, Adam and Eve, He put them in the Garden to take care of it. They were sure they would live happily ever after. Isn't that what we all want: to live happily ever after, to find a faith that will make us feel good…that will give us peace?

Adam and Eve lived in a perfect garden and had a stress-free existence. Their Father God wanted to walk and talk with them forever, and He gave them only one rule: Don't eat the fruit from the tree of the knowledge of good and evil.

All was well in this tropical paradise for a season, but then the day came when Eve listened to the flattering serpent who told her to pay no attention to what God had said about "the tree" and about the rules. "Do what you want to do," he encouraged. "Be your own person. Don't you know that when you eat that fruit you will be even more wise than you are right now? This is miracle food!" Even though Eve knew that God was in the Garden, she took a chance that He wouldn't notice, and she ate the fruit. She not only partook, but she also got Adam involved. Perhaps she wanted to make sure that if she got in trouble, she wouldn't be alone. Adam apparently didn't think about it or even ask God about it; he just ate as Eve instructed. Even though she and Adam both knew God personally, and were close to Him in the Garden, they yielded to temptation and disobeyed.

Consulting the Map

Like Adam and Eve, many of us think God doesn't see everything we do, maybe doesn't even care. Read the following scripture passages to determine what God's Word says about whether or not God notices our sin. Record the lesson you learn from each verse.

Jeremiah 23:24

_____

_____

Psalm 139:8

_____

_____

Proverbs 15:3

_____

_____

These verses show us that God is everywhere. This concept is usually referred to as God's _omnipresence,_ although this term never actually occurs in Scripture.

It is human nature to want to hide when we know we have done something wrong. Read the following scripture passages to see how God feels about our attempt to hide our sin. Record the results of trying to hide.

Proverbs 28:13

_____

_____

Isaiah 29:15

_____

_____

*Then the man and his wife heard the sound of the LORD God as he was walking
in the garden in the cool of the day, and they hid from the LORD God among the
trees of the garden.*

—Genesis 3:8

Besides being disobedient and suddenly becoming aware of their nakedness, both Adam and Eve were deceptive. When God came looking for them in the Garden, they were afraid and hid, in hopes that He wouldn't find them. And when the all-seeing God asked them if they had eaten from the one tree that was forbidden, they responded like children caught with their hands in the cookie jar. Adam tried to avoid responsibility by putting the blame on Eve: *"The woman you put here with me — she gave me some fruit from the tree, and I ate it"* (Genesis 3:12).

Eve wasn't much better. She avoided honest responsibility by saying quickly and cleverly: *"The serpent deceived me, and I ate"* (Genesis 3:13). Can't you just hear her saying, "Surely it wasn't *my* fault! Shouldn't we always be seeking self-improvement?" Eve tried to evade the truth by putting the blame on the serpent instead of saying, "I did it. It's my fault. I'm sorry."

Because they had disobeyed God and were deceptive — as God said to Adam: *"Because you listened to your wife and ate from the tree"* (Genesis 3:17) — they were punished and driven from the Garden of Eden. To protect the entrance to the Garden, God placed the first cherubim mentioned in the Bible as a guardian.

*After he drove the man out, he placed on the east side of the Garden of Eden
cherubim and a flaming sword flashing back and forth to guard the way to the
tree of life.*

—Genesis 3:24

Because Adam and Eve disobeyed God's simple and clear command and then tried to cover their tracks in deception, God expelled them from their place of perfect peace.

However, that is not the end of the story. Even at the beginning of the history of the world, when God was pronouncing judgment on Adam and Eve, He also gave them a promise. Speaking to the serpent, He said:

*"And I will put enmity between you and the woman, and between your offspring
and hers; he will crush your head, and you will strike his heel."*

—Genesis 3:15

On that dark day, the first day that sin entered the world and it seemed as if all had been lost, a glimmer of hope shone through. A Savior would come one day, who, although the serpent would strike His heel — a temporary blow — He would strike the Serpent's head — a fatal, crushing blow.

Consulting the Map

We have all sinned and fallen short of God's glory. When we sin, there is a right way and a wrong way to deal with it. When Adam and Eve disobeyed God, they tried to hide their sin. Let's look to God's Word to determine the correct response to sin and the results of that response.

*If we (see Ezra 10:11):*_____

*Then He (see 1 John 1:9):*_____

*We will (see Ezekiel 18:22):*_____

*And He will give us (see Acts 26:18):*_____

Ezra 10:11 says to *confess your sin to the LORD, the God of your ancestors, and do what he demands. Separate yourselves from the people of the land and from these pagan women* **(NLT). How would you apply this "separation" concept to your life today?**

_____

_____

Are there some things that tempt you from which you need to separate yourself? List them here.

_____

_____

_____

Write a prayer to the Lord incorporating the above elements of God's promises and committing yourself to separation from the things that tempt you.

_____

_____

_____

For Us in Today's World

How about the rest of us? Are we in a mess today? Are we looking for God to bail us out? Are we hoping to find Him in some mythical garden? Has someone told us that when we ask the Lord into our life things will suddenly become a rose garden?

My favorite hymn as a child was "In the Garden" by C. Austin Miles. Because my father's store, where we lived, was set right on the sidewalk and our yard was the cracked cement where the one gas pump had settled in, I always longed for green grass and some flowers. I tried planting things in the dirt next to the side of the store and was grateful that at least the hollyhocks kept coming back each year. Once I tried to transplant some lady's slippers from the woods near my grandmother's house, but they soon died, leaving nary a footprint in the soil. I often pictured living in a garden, and I loved novels where the heroine looked out her window onto manicured English hedges, cool fountains, and magnolia blossoms.

Singing the words, "I come to the garden alone while the dew is still on the roses," became a spiritual experience for me, knowing that He would walk with me and talk with me and tell me I was His own. As I would sing in church and look out the window to our shabby brown store across the street, I wished for flowers. I wanted to walk and talk with God in a garden where the dew was still on the roses.

A young lady wrote me a touching letter composed in a public rose garden. She had serious family problems, so she took her Bible in hand and drove to the garden. As she sat quietly praying and reading the book of Psalms, a peace came over her, and she felt the presence of the Lord. She could have done the same thing at home, but for her, removing herself from the scene of agitation allowed her to look for God in the garden. And He walked with her, and He talked with her, and He told her she was His own. This woman still has unsolved difficulties, but she knows that there is a garden where she can meet her Lord.

Consulting the Map

Like the woman in the preceding story, many people find God's peace in a garden. Jesus went to the garden to pray (see John 18:1–2). Addressing these verses, *Barnes' Notes on the New Testament* has this to say:

For what purpose he went there is not declared, but it is probable that it was for retirement and prayer. He had no home in the city, and he sought this place, away from the bustle and confusion of the capital, for private communion with God.[1]

Every Christian should have someplace — be it a grove, a room, or a garden — where they may be alone and offer their devotions to God. In what places do you find private communion with God?

Read Luke 22:39–46.
What did Jesus experience while praying in the Garden of Gethsemane?

_____

_____

_____

What have you experienced when focused in prayer in your own "private place"?

_____

_____

_____

If you have not experimented with going to the "garden," try spending time in prayer in some private spot near your home.

In the beginning, God walked and talked with Adam and Eve in the lush Garden of Eden. He asked for simple obedience and honesty in return for fellowship and food. Given a free mind, they made the wrong choices. It seems that even being in perfect circumstances didn't guarantee that they would choose correctly. Beautiful surroundings weren't enough. Lack of stress wasn't enough. Being in God's presence didn't automatically make them turn away from sin. They both disobeyed and were deceptive.

How many of us feel if we could only get our house in order; if we could get the lawn mowed and the roses to bloom; if we didn't have to go to work each day; if we didn't have those children who messed things up; if our environment were only perfect; if God was walking in our own backyard where we could see Him in the cool of the day, we could really live for Him? We could pray out loud; we could write psalms; we could sing like the angels.

God doesn't ask for drama and displays; He wants simple obedience to His directions, and honesty, not deception. Our circumstances may never be anywhere close to perfection, but God can create for us a garden of rest in our hearts, when we choose His approval over the temptations of the world.

Let's not wait for that great someday when we get it all together and have time for God. Let's meet Him in the garden of our hearts right now and let Him restore our souls.

Trip Journal

From the beginning of Scripture, we can see the basic spirit of disobedience in human nature. With this thought in mind, answer the following questions in your Trip Journal.

1.   How did Eve disobey God?
2.   Was Adam any better?
3.   Where did he fail?
4.   How does this apply to your own life?
5.   Why do you think people are deceptive?
6.   What circumstance last led you to skirt the truth?
7.   Do you feel we are born deceptive?
8.   Why was Eve deceptive with God?
9.   How do you handle your children when they lie?
10. Have you ever felt banished from the Garden? Separated from God? When and why? Are you still in that place?

LESSON 3

In the Fields

Read Genesis 4.

As we leave the Garden of Eden and catch the last glimpse of the cherubim at the gate and the *flaming sword flashing back and forth to guard the way to the tree of life* (Genesis 3:24), we find ourselves in barren fields where thorns and thistles grow. The roadmap seems to have come to a dead end. Adam, banished to painful toil for the rest of his life, was working by the sweat of his brow with his son Cain, while Abel was tending the sheep.

For God's People in Bible Times

In Genesis 4, God called for the first recorded sacrifice from His people. Adam's son Abel, in obedience to God, brought an animal from the firstborn of his flock, and God was pleased. Because Cain, strong-willed and rebellious, brought fruit and did not make the expected blood sacrifice, God was displeased and let him know it.

Consulting the Map

Carefully read Genesis 4:6–7, and if possible, compare several different versions. (If you are doing this as a group study, have different members read several versions out loud to absorb the full implications of these verses.)

Based on what you read, what was God's desire for Cain?

_____

_____

Now read 2 Peter 3:9.

How do God's desires compare in these two verses, one from the Old Testament and one from the New?

_____

_____

God attempted to give Cain guidance and direction to correct his bad actions and attitude. How did Cain respond to God's rebuke?

_____

_____

Did he take responsibility for his own actions, or did he take it out on others?

_____

According to Proverbs 19:3, who is responsible when someone sins?

_____

How do you respond to corrective action when you have done something wrong?

_____

_____

Based on what we have read here, what would be the best course of action when we sin?

_____

_____

Cain, in his anger at being rebuked, struck out and killed his brother, Abel. When God asked Cain directly what had happened to Abel, he avoided the honest answer by instead deceptively asking, _"Am I my brother's keeper?"_ (Genesis 4:9). In other words, Cain said, "How should I know where he is?!" Cain had inherited the deceptive spirit of his parents.

God knew what Cain had done to Abel, and He was disheartened by Cain's deception. God could have killed Cain, but He chose a punishment more severe: God banished Cain from his fertile fields and said, _"You will be a restless wanderer on the earth"_ (Genesis 4:12).

Cain cried out to God, _"My punishment is more than I can bear. Today you are driving me from the land, and I will be hidden from your presence; I will be a restless wanderer on the earth, and whoever finds me will kill me"_ (Genesis 4:13–14).

Like Cain, we all make choices, and we often suffer as a result of the choices other people make. Cain made a choice that displeased the Lord, as did his parents. These choices put him in a place from where he cried out, _"My punishment is more than I can bear"_ (Genesis 4:13). Often the results of our choices and the choices of those around us feel like more than we can bear.

Read the following scripture passages to see what God has to say about suffering. Are we the only ones who suffer? How does God respond?

Exodus 3:7

_____

_____

Psalm 31:22

_____

_____

Romans 8:18

_____

_____

2 Corinthians 4:8

_____

_____

Cain felt that God had given him more than he could bear. Many times we cry out to God with the same response. Read 1 Corinthians 10:13. Write out God's promise to us from this verse.

_____

_____

God assured Cain that he would not be killed, so to set him apart and protect him, God put the "mark of Cain" upon him (see Genesis 4:15).

For Us in Today's World

Do you ever feel that you are wandering in the wilderness, that God has forgotten you — if He ever knew you in the first place?! He has promised that _he will never leave you nor forsake you_ (Deuteronomy 31:6).

God met with Cain and Abel in the field where animals were grazing and grain was growing. What better place to be close to God and admire His handiwork than in the field where God's gardening plan of reaping what we sow is in such clear evidence?! We see that mighty oaks grow out of little acorns, and apple trees don't grow bananas. Without God there would be no explanation for how a tiny pansy seed knows it must grow up to be a pansy and not a petunia; no chance that on occasion a grain of wheat might become an ear of corn.

Let's stop and think right now. What are you sowing? What are you putting in your mind? Are you reading God's Word and Christian literature? Or are you filling your mind with trivia and trash? Garbage in, garbage out. What are you planting in the hearts of your mate and close friends? Are you inserting kind and gracious words that will produce positive responses? What seeds are you placing in the fertile minds of your little ones? How embarrassing it can sometimes be to hear our own words repeated back to us out of the mouths of babes. We do reap what we sow — God's principles work in people as well as in the fields.

Consulting the Map

Today's reading from Genesis talks about sacrifices. We will learn more about them later on in this journey. But for us today, what does God's Word tell us is most important?

Read the following verses from both the Old and New Testaments and record what each says is God's priority.

1 Samuel 15:22

_____

_____

Isaiah 1:11, 16–17

_____

_____

Hosea 6:6

_____

_____

Matthew 9:13

_____

_____

Matthew 12:7

_____

_____

Like Cain, all of us toil in fields with rocks and other discomforts — even in our chosen "fields." Based on the scriptures above, how are we to respond to these impediments in our lives?

_____

_____

Easton's Illustrated Bible Dictionary defines _mercy_ as compassion for the miserable and a "Christian grace."[1]

Read Matthew 5:7 and Matthew 18:33–35. According to God's Word, why is it important that we show mercy to those "rocks" in our field?

_____

_____

Think of someone in your "field" who represents a "rock" to you. Write a prayer here asking God to give you mercy for that person the next time you encounter them.

_____

_____

_____

Trip Journal

Throughout Scripture we find that the sins of the father are carried into the next generation. Think about that concept as you answer the following questions in your Trip Journal.

1. How did Cain first disobey God?
2. What emotion caused Cain to turn on his brother, Abel?
3. When looking at Adam, Eve, and Cain, what consistency of attitude and behavior do you see?
4. Which of these traits have you experienced in your own life?
5. Why did Cain ask, "Am I my brother's keeper?"
6. Is "doing your own thing" ever positive?

LESSON 4

On a Walk with God

Read Genesis 5:18–27.

Many articles are written each year on physical fitness and the value of exercise. We know that walking and jogging increase our blood circulation. So no doubt, exercise is a must for "other people." We plan to join them for an early morning walk — someday. A few of us even buy cute jogging clothes to tuck in our suitcase so that if we get an urge to run while we are in a distant city, we'll be prepared. How impressed we all will be as in this lesson we meet Enoch, a man who didn't just do an occasional sit-up but who "walked with God 300 years!"

For God's People in Bible Times

Enoch, the father of Methuselah, was an obedient and godly man. *Altogether, Enoch lived 365 years. Enoch walked with God; then he was no more, because God took him away* (Genesis 5:23–24).

Enoch *walked with God*, and because he had obeyed and had not been deceptive, God took him to be with Him in paradise without experiencing a physical death.

Consulting the Map

In our previous two lessons, the lead characters were all disobedient and deceptive, and they were punished. But Enoch lived according to God's plans — *Enoch walked with God* — and was rewarded. As a Christian, each of us desires reward rather than punishment. Let's look at what is involved in "walking with God."

Read the following scriptures to determine what we are responsible for in order to "walk with God" as Enoch did. Enoch was taken to heaven as a result of his walk. What will be our reward?

	RESPONSIBILITY	REWARD
Deuteronomy 5:33	_____	_____
Deuteronomy 26:16–19	_____	_____
1 Kings 2:3	_____	_____
1 Kings 3:14	_____	_____
Jeremiah 6:16	_____	_____
Jeremiah 7:23	_____	_____
Ezekiel 11:20	_____	_____
Colossians 1:9–14	_____	_____

In defining the word *walk,* the *International Standard Bible Encyclopedia* has this to say: "Aside from its frequent occurrence in the usual sense, the word 'walk' is used figuratively of conduct and of spiritual states."[1] Depending on the version of the Bible you are using, your translation may use the word *live.*

Although Enoch lived in a society of sinful souls, he walked so closely with God that he was able to be in the world but not of the world. Because the people feared death, Enoch became a symbol of a positive afterlife.

Consulting the Map

Read John 17:15–19.

In your own words, explain how we can be in the world but not of the world.

_____

_____

_____

Enoch was a model of the afterlife. What about your "walk" is a model of the Christian life?

_____

_____

_____

Are there any things in your life that would prevent people from knowing that you are "not of this world?" From the list below, check off the things in your life that you would like to correct, and add any that the Lord brings to your mind.

- ○ **Unforgiveness**
- ○ **Anger**
- ○ **Controlling nature**
- ○ **Cheating**
- ○ **Lack of peace**
- ○ **Too much, or inappropriate television**
- ○ **Drugs or alcohol**
- ○ **Not keeping promises**
- ○ **Other:**_____

Rest Stop

Write a prayer to God asking for His help in overcoming these areas, so that while you are in this world, others will see something different about you and know that you are not of this world. Repeat this prayer out loud and continue to pray that you will be a model of the Christian life.

_____
_____
_____
_____
_____
_____

By faith Enoch was translated that he should not see death; and was not found, because God had translated him: for before his translation he had this testimony, that he pleased God. But without faith it is impossible to please him: for he that cometh to God must believe that he is, and that he is a rewarder of them that diligently seek him.

—Hebrews 11:5–6, KJV

For Us in Today's World

How about you and me? Are we earnestly seeking God? Are we walking with God as Enoch did? Are we so close to God that our very steps are going uphill toward heaven? Are we so identified with Jesus that God looks down and can't tell us apart? Could God say of us, "That person is so perfectly in tune with Me that I must bring him up to fellowship with Me and seat him in heavenly places"? That's how God saw Enoch, as a friend so close to His divine thinking that they were two hearts that beat as one.

Sometimes we find that relationship with another human being in which we often know exactly what the other one is thinking. My daughters, Marita and Lauren, and I are "tuned in" to each other. We are of one mind; we walk together. Whenever they are with me, they can take one look at a meeting room where I am to speak and see it with my eyes. They put themselves in my position automatically because they've been so close to me for so long. Neither one has to stand and say, "What would Mother want changed or moved?" They just take action as I would; they can see with my eyes. When I am speaking, they sense when I'm too hot, when the room is too stuffy, or when I need a drink of water. We have joked for years that, since they have heard my testimony hundreds of times, if I were to drop dead in the middle of it, either one of them could step over my body and continue my life story without missing a beat. We are not just related by blood — we are close in spirit. We have not only traveled together — we have "walked" together.

God wants us to have that kind of fellowship with Him. He wants our relationship with Him to be deeper than just a born-again experience. He wants us to be of one mind in the Spirit — not just strolling down the path to heaven, but walking with Jesus.

I used to tell my Bible classes when they would tend to elevate me as their leader, "As long as I keep showing up each week, you'll know I'm not yet perfected, for when God sees me as 'like unto Himself,' He will snatch me up to heaven, and no one will know why or how I disappeared. I'll be like a spiritual Mary Poppins floating off into the future!"

Enoch was so close to God that the Almighty couldn't leave him here with the rest of us; He translated him, whisked him away. How about us? Are we so in step with the Lord that our feet can barely stay on the ground? Are we one wink away from eternity? Do we tread so in tune to God's plan for our life that there's only one set of footprints in the sand?

The late Bill Bright, founder of Campus Crusade for Christ, called this process "spiritual breathing," inhaling and exhaling with the very breath of God.

Oswald Chambers also put it clearly when he wrote:

> It is a painful business to get through into the stride of God, it means getting your second wind spiritually. In learning to walk with God there is always the difficulty of getting into His stride; but when we have gotten into it, the only characteristic that manifests itself is the life of God. The individual man is

lost sight of in his personal union with God, and the stride and the power of God alone are manifested.[2]

Are we that in stride with God? Or is He several steps ahead of us? Has He already turned the corner and disappeared from sight? Walking with God is not being cheerfully chummy with Christ, but being so close to Him that we lay our head on His bosom and breathe in and out to God's rhythm.

How do we get to know Christ that well? The same way we get to know anyone. By spending time with Him. When a new neighbor moves in, many times we make our initial judgment on their status and taste by observing their furniture as it comes out of the moving van. But we don't really know them. To get to know our neighbors we have to walk next door, introduce ourselves, and spend some time with them.

It's the same with God; we have to spend time with Him. We all want to know Him, but we don't take the time to study His Word, to feel the power of His presence, to get in stride with Him. Let's get acquainted with Him today so we can walk with Him in stride tomorrow.

Enoch's testimony was that *he pleased God.* Let's hope the same can be said of us.

Trip Journal

1.   Do you have a place of retreat, a garden in your life, where you can go to walk and talk with God?

2.   Where is it?

3.   How often do you go there?

4.   How do you feel when you're there?

5.   Do you have that same feeling with God that Enoch had?

6.   How much time do you spend each day in Bible study?

7.   How much time do you spend each day in prayer?

8.   How could you improve your "spiritual breathing"?

9.   How could you get "in stride" with God?

In the Rain

Read Genesis 6–8.

From the time I was a child, I knew the story of Noah and the ark. I knew that the animals came two by two, that it rained a lot, and that a rainbow appeared to end it all. People today are still fascinated by this story. In August 1986, former astronaut James Irwin went to eastern Turkey to climb the 17,000-foot Mt. Ararat in search of the lost ark. Is it really there? Is this story fact or fiction? What does the Bible say? As we move on in our journey toward God, we come to the time of Noah. Better pull out your raincoat and umbrella. It's beginning to sprinkle.

For God's People in Bible Times

In the times of Noah, God saw that His highest creation, man, had become incredibly evil: *The LORD was grieved that he had made man on the earth, and his heart was filled with pain* (Genesis 6:6).

Consulting the Map

Many people today want to believe that God is a god who is far off, some mystical being without any feelings toward mankind.

Read Genesis 1:27 and 5:1.
Based on these verses, do you think God is a being who has no feelings? Why or why not?

_____

_____

Read the following verses. For each, note the feelings that are attributed to God, Jesus, and the Holy Spirit.

*Deuteronomy 31:16–17

_____

_____

*Isaiah 63:10

_____

_____

*Isaiah 65:12

_____

_____

*Psalm 7:11–12

_____

_____

Luke 10:21

_____

_____

Luke 19:41

_____

John 11:33

_____

John 11:35

_____

*John 14:21

_____

_____

John 15:11

_____

_____

Reread the verses marked with an asterisk (*) and note what actions bring about a negative emotion in God and which bring out a positive one.

NEGATIVE	POSITIVE
_____	_____
_____	_____
_____	_____
_____	_____
_____	_____

What is God's response to us based on our actions?

NEGATIVE	POSITIVE
_____	_____
_____	_____
_____	_____
_____	_____
_____	_____

Which do you want from God?

_____

_____

Write a prayer asking God to help you keep His commands.

_____

_____

_____

_____

Noah found favor with God because he, like Enoch, was _a righteous man, blameless among the people of his time, and he walked with God_ (Genesis 6:9). From what I read about Noah in the Scriptures, it seems to me he was a deep, thoughtful, introspective, and analytical man. Whatever he did, he usually did perfectly.

God talked to Noah and said, _"I am going to put an end to all people, for the earth is filled with violence because of them. I am surely going to destroy both them and the earth"_ (Genesis 6:13).

God then gave Noah explicit directions on how to build the ark, the vessel that was to be his salvation. *Noah did everything just as God commanded him* (Genesis 6:22).

The rains came for forty days and forty nights and then finally stopped. At that time, Noah sent out a dove to see if the waters had receded, but the dove returned because there was no dry land for it to rest upon. Noah waited seven more days and then sent out the dove again. This time the dove came back with a fresh olive leaf. In seven more days, Noah sent the dove out again. This time it did not return, and when God told him it was safe, Noah left the ark and began a new life.

The first thing Noah did when he left the ark on Mount Ararat was to build an altar and sacrifice some animals and birds in praise to God for saving him and his family. *The LORD smelled the pleasing aroma* (Genesis 8:21) and pledged to never destroy the earth by flood again. He made a covenant with Noah — a covenant for all generations to come (see Genesis 9:9–11) — because He knew he could trust him.

> *"I have set my rainbow in the clouds, and it will be the sign of the covenant between me and the earth. Whenever I bring clouds over the earth and the rainbow appears in the clouds, I will remember my covenant between me and you and all living creatures of every kind. Never again will the waters become a flood to destroy all life."*
>
> —Genesis 9:13–15

Noah walked and talked with God, and because of his honest obedience, he and his family and future generations were saved.

For Us in Today's World

I've often wondered how I might have responded if God had told me to go home and build an ark. Would I have done *just as God commanded?* Or would I have argued? "God, You know I can't hammer straight! I've never been good at mechanical things. And it's not even raining! Don't You see I live in the desert of southern California? Plus, what will people think of me? If I start building a big ark in the front yard, the neighbors will be furious. They already made the man next door remove his motorboat from the driveway where he had settled it on blocks for the winter! What would they do if I were to build an ark?"

Even if I were willing to build the ark, would my strong willful nature want to do it God's way? Would I obey His instructions? I'm sure I'd have better ideas: "Couldn't we have more windows? I like a view, and I like to see outside. Could we paint it blue, give the boat a name, and wallpaper the bathroom? There won't be a bathroom? Then count me out!"

I've never wanted to do anything exactly as someone else had in mind, and naturally, with the changes I want to make, I always feel I'm improving on their plans — not making things worse. One night when my husband, Fred, and I were eating out, he asked me what I was thinking about. I hesitated to tell him I was redesigning the floor plan of the restaurant and unconsciously constructing a wall to hide the dish room that was in my clear view. When I mentioned this dubious talent of mine to my daughter Lauren, she laughed and told me she herself had just gone to look at a mini-mall still under construction to see if she would like to open a new coin store there. As she talked with the builder, she could see he obviously needed her help in laying out a floor plan that would be more functional. She pointed out some necessary changes and obvious improvements that she felt needed to be done whether or not she rented space. By the time she left, the poor confused man was busily reviewing his blueprints and modifying his plans.

What would Lauren and I have done if God had told us to build an ark and to use His directions — *without changing them?* Thankfully, Noah wasn't like us! Noah was willing to meet God in the rain, to obey His instructions, and to do *everything just as God commanded him.* He didn't argue with God or insist on his own way.

Consulting the Map

In Noah's day, God spoke to His people in ways that seem very plain and clear to us today. Read the following verses and note how God communicated in each passage.

Exodus 3:2

_____

Exodus 32:7

_____

Deuteronomy 10:4

_____

1 Kings 19:11–13

_____

Daniel 5:5

_____

John 12:28

_____

Most of us today wish that God would write His will on the wall for us, send an angel, speak through a burning bush, or simply shout it from the heavens. It would be much easier to follow His commands if they were that clear. God does still speak to us today, although most of the time He does not use such obvious methods. So how do we hear God's voice today? How can we know His commands?

Read the following passages and note what each tells us about hearing God's voice and what that means for us today.

John 10:4, 16, 27; Isaiah 30:21; 1 Kings 19:12

_____

_____

Ecclesiastes 12:11

_____

_____

Deuteronomy 17:19; Psalm 119:97–100

_____

_____

If we want to hear God's voice, we must first know Him intimately, for His voice is soft. We must seek wise counsel and we must know God's Word. One day a lady asked me how I knew if the voice I was hearing was really God's voice. I told her that when I hear that still, small voice in my heart telling me to do something for someone else, and it is something I do not want to do or is not within my nature, I usually understand that that prompting is from God. I have found that He doesn't usually have to tell me to go to Nordstrom's for a big sale — but He does have to tell me to make a large contribution to charity or go talk to someone toward whom I have been harboring unforgiveness in my heart.

> *By faith Noah, when warned about things not yet seen, in holy fear built an ark to save his family. By his faith he condemned the world and became heir of the righteousness that comes by faith.*
>
> —Hebrews 11:7

Is God asking you to build an ark today — to do something you don't understand, to prepare for a future you can't foresee? Is God telling you to spend more time now building relationships with your children in order to "save" your family when the rains come? Is He asking you to prepare for bad weather while the sun is shining? Is He begging to spend time with you, while you claim to be too busy? Have you been looking up through the clouds and shouting at God, "Don't rain on my parade!"?

Noah listened to God in the sunshine and prepared for the stormy weather. And when the rains came, Noah *continued* to listen to God and remained faithful. Oswald Chambers wrote:

> At times God puts us through the discipline of darkness to teach us to heed Him.... Watch where God puts you into darkness, and when you are there keep your mouth shut.... Darkness is the time to listen.... When you are in the dark, listen, and God will give you a very precious message for someone else when you get into the light.[1]

Let's spend time with God today; tomorrow may be too late. There are no instant arks; they take time to build. Let's get to know the Master Builder so He'll be able to keep us afloat when the rain comes. He's no fair-weather friend, but He wants to spend time with us now, in the present!

Shakespeare wrote:

> There is a tide in the affairs of men,
>
> Which, taken at the flood, leads on to fortune;
>
> Omitted, all the voyage of their life
>
> Is bound in shallows and in miseries....
>
> We must take the current when it serves.
>
> Or lose our ventures.

—Julius Caesar, Act 4, Scene 3

Don't be one of those Christians who are "bound in shallows and in miseries." Get to know God in the warmth of the sunshine so that you'll be singing when the rain comes. God wants to save you and me as He did Noah. Don't miss the boat!

Trip Journal

God warned the people of Noah's time to turn from their wicked ways and look fully to Him. Record your answers to the following questions in your Trip Journal.

1. What behavior did the people in Noah's day exhibit?
2. At what point in your life has God ever given you a warning?
3. Did you take His advice?
4. What happened?
5. One principle from God that runs throughout the Bible is that when God gives clear directions, we have the choice to either follow Him or disobey Him. When we follow Him, He blesses us, but when we disobey, He punishes us. How can you see this principle being applied in Noah's situation?

Scenic Overlook

One summer evening Elaine was scheduled to share her testimony at a friend's poolside supper party. Just as the guests were arriving, the skies parted and rain poured onto the patio. Tables and chairs were quickly dragged into the small living room that soon became so filled with furniture that there was no room for the people.

The resourceful hostess, seeing no change in the weather, decided to move the party and Elaine's performance to the garage. "This was no finished room," Elaine explained, wide-eyed. "It was just a dirty old garage with a wheel-less Dodge up on jacks. Water was pouring in under the doors and splashing up against the far wall. It began to look like an oil-laden swamp."

Elaine stood at a podium that was placed over the drain in the garage floor and began to tell her life story to a sad-looking group who well may have wondered what they were doing listening to Bible verses in a garage with water swirling around their feet.

At the conclusion, the hostess, seemingly oblivious to the dampened spirits and wet shoes, asked each guest to take off their limp name tag and put an X on it if they had asked the Lord into their life that night. After the guests "swam" back out to their cars to leave, Elaine was too embarrassed to look at the tags, but the hostess counted the decisions and found that despite the rain several people had met the Lord.

Because Elaine had been obedient in a bizarre set of circumstances, twelve searching people found God in a garage in the rain.

LESSON 6

At the Tower

Read Genesis 11:1–9.

So many of us wish we could have a fresh start in life. "If only I could begin again!" we sigh. We want a new roadmap that takes us in a different direction.

Would we do it all better if we had another chance? Or would we perhaps make even bigger mistakes? God the Father gave His people a new beginning. When He created the world, He stepped back and said, "That's good." But He gave Adam and Eve a will of their own, and even though they had walked with Him in the Garden, they both disobeyed and brought sin into the world.

After watching several generations pass, the Father looked at His children in disappointment and had to admit, "This is a sorry lot."

If you are a parent, perhaps you've had similar feelings when your offspring made choices that disappointed you. Perhaps at some point you've even wondered how a sane, sober, conservative person like yourself could have produced a child who wears green punk hair and a gold earring, or one who's still in school at thirty-two years old, or one who has returned home unmarried with a new baby. Even though we can't really compare these frustrations with God's disappointment in the days of Noah, perhaps you can have some understanding of God's anguish as He sighed and wished He had never created mankind in the first place. Yet in the midst of all of this wickedness on the earth, there stood Noah, a righteous man, and God spared him to give the world a second chance.

We are now leaving Noah there on Mount Ararat with his own personal rainbow curled around his shoulder, and we are heading forward to a city where we will find people with short memories and little gratitude toward God.

For God's People in Bible Times

As with any difficult experience, the impact of the crisis decreases with the passage of time. Noah's descendants soon forgot that God desired obedience, honesty, and humility among His people — and the consequences when they lived in disobedience to Him. This new group of people settled in an area near latter-day Babylon, about fifty miles south of today's Baghdad. As they structured their new civilization, one of their first thoughts was to build a monument to themselves to show their power and authority. This tower was not an altar to God, but to themselves.

> *"Come, let us build ourselves a city, with a tower that reaches to the heavens, so that we may make a name for ourselves and not be scattered over the face of the whole earth." But the LORD came down to see the city and the tower that the men were building.*
>
> —Genesis 11:4–5

> *So the LORD scattered them from there over all the earth, and they stopped building the city. That is why it was called Babel — because there the LORD confused the language of the whole world. From there the LORD scattered them over the face of the whole earth.*
>
> —Genesis 11:8–9

Although the word *Babel* means "gate of God," our God knew this tower was not a doorway to His holiness but instead a step toward the reverence of humanity.

Consulting the Map

Read Genesis 11:4.

What character trait did the people exhibit in their desire to build the tower?

_____

Babylon was a proud city, thought to be the "gate of God" — yet even it faced desolation. Let's look at what God's Word says about pride and the true gateway to God.

Look up the following verses that address pride to see how God feels about it.

Proverbs 16:18

_____

Isaiah 13:11

_____

Jeremiah 49:16

_____

Malachi 4:1

_____

Based on what you have learned in these verses, do you think God treated the city of Babylon in a way that is consistent with His Word? Explain.

_____

_____

_____

Pride and humility are opposites. If _pride goes before destruction_, what happens to the humble? Read the following verses to confirm your answer.

Psalm 18:27	**Proverbs 3:34**	**Habakkuk 2:4**
Isaiah 57:15	**1 Peter 5:5–6**	**1 John 2:16–17**

_____

_____

_____

Based on the above passages of Scripture, whom does God say He will save?

_____

The Babylonians thought that they were building a gate to God. Read John 10:9. What is the true gateway to God?

_____

_____

For Us in Today's World

Isn't it fascinating today to realize that many of our twenty-first-century world problems are centered in the same area of Babylon as we read about in Scripture? In years past, who would have thought that the United States would have troops in Baghdad? The country of Iraq seemed so distant at that time, and yet, here we are rebuilding it today.

When I watched the statue of Saddam Hussein being pushed off its pedestal — right there on television — I couldn't help but connect this event with biblical Babylon, when the people of that time were also building monuments to themselves.

In my lifetime, I have seen how many godly people with good intentions can become overly impressed by their own spirituality, especially when they are constantly surrounded by adoring audiences. The world is looking for a leader to follow, a god to guide them, a benevolent dictator to keep control. How easy it is, when sensing the adulation of the crowd, to see oneself as sovereign. But God's eyesight has not dimmed. When He observes a ministry that has shifted its attention and worship from Him to its human leader, He can still confuse its language and scatter that ministry right before our eyes.

Consulting the Map

While we understand that God tears down the proud and builds up the humble, still so many "leaders" — who may have started out with humble, pure motives — become so proud that they even build monuments to themselves.

According to 1 Samuel 8:19–20, how can this take place?

_____

_____

Along the same lines, according to Matthew 20:25–28, what did the Jewish people in Christ's time expect from the Messiah, and what did they actually get?

_____

_____

Read James 3:1.

_____

How does this verse fit into our discussion of pride, humility, and leaders building monuments to themselves?

_____

_____

Even if you are not a "leader" in the strict sense of the word, what can you learn from this discussion?

_____

_____

_____

What a lesson there is in this brief passage of Scripture for those of us who are visible as leaders: We must keep our eyes on the Lord and not on ourselves so that we will build ministries for Him and not monuments to us — mere human beings.

At the time of the Jim Jones mass suicide, Rabbi Harold M. Schulweis wrote in the _Los Angeles Times_ that we tend to "set charismatic leaders apart, idealizing some as saints or condemning others as devils." Often the leaders who are "saints" one day become the fallen ones the next. The rabbi went on to say:

> Overnight, leaders who have been raised to the heights are cast to the depth. We would be less taken aback by such contradictions if we were to follow the wisdom of biblical monotheism, for the Scripture knows the mischief that follows from either idealizing or demonizing God's creatures.
>
> Scripture warns us that "there is no righteous person who does good and does not sin" [Ecclesiastes 7:20]. Its respected tales of flawed patriarchs, princes, priests and prophets illustrate the tragic folly of idolatry.
>
> But we mortals do need heroes; we seek out figures of exemplary strength and wisdom. Yet we must be reminded that the creatures of God are limited, and that adulation often becomes a temptation to mount the tower and assume the power of divinity.[1]

Let us limited creatures be reminded that we aren't God and that we don't have any special license to sin just because we may have "given up so much for God." We must take care not to be tempted to "mount the tower and assume the power of divinity."

Trip Journal

1. Has there ever been a time in your life when you have wanted to start over again? If so, when was it, and why did you need a fresh start?

2. If you were God, what would you think of the world today — especially as compared to the time of Noah? If God were to look for a righteous family, would He find one?

3. Noah's family saw God's miraculous hand of deliverance on their lives. Even so, they slipped back into their old ways after the Flood. Why do you suppose they did this?

4. The people who built the Tower of Babel had "positive" motives: "Let's make a monument to ourselves." "We've worked hard — let's build something to remind future generations of our accomplishments. Let's leave a legacy!" When the Lord came down from heaven to look at what they were building, why was He displeased? What did He do to stop the building?

5. Have you ever built any monument to yourself? Have you ever created a scheme to cause others to notice your accomplishments? How might God be pleased or displeased with the motives of your heart?

LESSON 7

In the Wilderness

Read Genesis 11:27–32.

In my early days of Bible study, I skipped genealogies. I didn't care who begat whom or in what order, but as I became a more serious student, I saw how important it was to follow a family line, to trace their inherited characteristics, both bad and good. During the writing of my book *Your Personality Tree*, I spent time interviewing my relatives, revisiting childhood haunts and homes, reflecting in the cemetery, and analyzing family personalities from the past. As I became enthralled with my own family background, I had a new desire to trace the traits of God's family and examine their personality tree. As you think about your own family tree, come with me and meet Abram. We'll trace his lineage and move with him through many experiences in the wilderness.

For God's People in Bible Times

From the three sons of Noah came all the nations of the earth. *Japheth's* descendants spread to many lands and spoke different languages. Through *Ham's* son Canaan came the Canaanites, and through *Ham's* son Cush came Nimrod, the mighty hunter. Nimrod was blessed of God, and his reign extended to Assyria where he built the city of Nineveh. From *Shem*, the oldest of the three, came some fascinating names such as Lud, Uz, Gether, and Mash. Later *Shem's* descendants included Nahor, his son Terah, and Terah's sons, Abram, Nahor, and Haran (the father of Lot).

Consulting the Map

Using your Bible concordance — or your current knowledge of the Bible (this one is easy) — list at least one other location in the Bible where a genealogy is listed. (If you are doing this as a group study, be sure that everyone has a chance to share the passages of Scripture they found.)

While most of us skip over the genealogies, there are so many included in the Bible that there must be a reason for them. Nothing in the Bible is simply a space filler.

Why do you think the genealogies are included?

_____

_____

_____

The *Barclay's Daily Study Bible* gives us some interesting background on the prevalence of genealogies in the Bible. Referring to the genealogy of Jesus found in Matthew, it says:

> It might seem to a modern reader that Matthew chose an extraordinary way in which to begin his gospel; and it might seem daunting to present right at the beginning a long list of names to wade through. But to a Jew this was the most natural, and the most interesting, and indeed the most essential way to begin the story of any man's life.
>
> The Jews were exceedingly interested in genealogies. Matthew calls this the book of the generation of Jesus Christ. That to the Jews was a common phrase; and it means the record of a man's lineage, with a few explanatory sentences, where such comment was necessary. In the Old Testament we frequently find lists of the generations of famous men. When Josephus, the great Jewish historian, wrote his own autobiography, he began it with his own pedigree, which, he tells us, he found in the public records.
>
> The reason for this interest in pedigrees was that the Jews set the greatest possible store on purity of lineage. If in any man there was the slightest mixture of foreign blood, he lost his right to be called a Jew, and a member of the people of God. A priest, for instance, was bound to produce an unbroken record of his pedigree stretching back to Aaron; and, if he married, the woman he married must produce her pedigree for at least five generations back.[1]

In about 1921 B.C., God spoke to peace-loving Abram, and said, *"Leave your country, your people and your father's household and go to the land I will show you"* (Genesis 12:1). God drew a roadmap for Abram, showing where he was and where he was to go.

Abram, who lived in Ur of the Chaldees, had no desire to move, but God promised him a reward for his obedience: *"I will make you into a great nation and I will bless you"* (Genesis 12:2). God also said that He would bless those who blessed Abram and curse those who cursed him (see Genesis 12:2–3).

The roadmap led to the wilderness at Haran:

Abram traveled through Mesopotamia to Haran, a place named after his brother. Obedient to God's command, Abram dutifully built an altar of sacrifice and praise to the Lord each time he moved.

The roadmap then led to the wilderness in Egypt:

From Haran, Abram took his ten-camel caravan to Palestine and later, because there was a famine, Abram decided on his own to go to Egypt with his beautiful wife. In fear that the Egyptians would desire Sarai and then kill him to obtain her, Abram asked her to say she was his sister. By this deceptive ploy, Abram hoped to save his own life. The Pharaoh did take Sarai to his palace and treated her "brother" Abram well, "for her sake."

When God inflicted disease upon the Pharaoh and his household because of Abram's deception, Pharaoh summoned Abram. *"What have you done to me?"* he said. *"Why didn't you tell me she was your wife? Why did you say, 'She is my sister' so that I took her to be my wife? Now then, here is your wife. Take her and go!"* (Genesis 12:18–19).

The roadmap led to the wilderness in Sodom and Gomorrah:

As Abram and his nephew Lot were in the wilderness together, quarrels broke out between their families. Abram, always the peacemaker, suggested they go in separate directions. Under God's inspiration, Abram selflessly gave Lot the first choice of the available land. Lot selected the fertile plain of the Jordan River, eventually settling near the city of Sodom (Genesis 13:8–13). This is the same Jordan River that exists in Israel today.

The lessons from Noah's day of God's destructive power over evil had long been forgotten. Because of their unrepentant attitude toward the sins of lust and homosexuality (Genesis 19:5–9), the people of Sodom and Gomorrah were guilty in God's sight, and He prepared to wipe out the wickedness of human beings once again. Abram, wanting to keep the peace and avoid disaster, begged God to spare the cities if there were ten righteous people in them. But God spared only Lot, his wife, and their two daughters by telling them to flee to the mountains and not look back. As God rained down burning sulphur from the heavens, Lot and his daughters obeyed as they fled, but Lot's wife turned to look back to the city — back to her past — and because of her disobedience, she was turned into a pillar of salt (Genesis 19:26).

Consulting the Map

Read the following verses and note what each verse says about looking back to the past.

Romans 6:6

_____

Ephesians 4:22

_____

Philippians 3:13

_____

Colossians 3:9

_____

2 Peter 1:9

_____

Are there things in your past that you keep taking out and looking at, things that are keeping you stuck where you are? Do you now realize that God wants you to let go of these things?

_____

_____

_____

Write a prayer asking God to help you relinquish the past. List the specific items with which you struggle.

_____

_____

_____

The roadmap led to the wilderness in Canaan:

Abram settled in Canaan, the land God gave him as an everlasting possession for him and his descendants. As patient Abram grew old and still had no children, he became doubtful of God's promise and cried out to God. The Lord made a covenant with Abram — he would be the father of the Hebrew race, his children would be as plentiful as the stars in the heavens, and they would inherit the land between the river of Egypt and the Euphrates River (see Genesis 15:5, 18).

God also predicted that Abram's descendants would be enslaved, in a land that was not their own, for 400 years before returning to possess their Promised Land (Genesis 15:13–16) The Scripture tells of the fulfillment of this prophecy in Exodus 1 and Psalm 105.

As the years went by and Abram and Sarai still had no promised children, Sarai became impatient and suggested to Abram, who was eighty-six years old by that time, that he have a child by her servant, Hagar. Humanly speaking, this seemed to make sense, but it was not God's plan. Hagar was as strong-willed as Sarai. And when two such strong-willed women live or work together, they will either agree, fight, or one will give in and put on a mask of peace. Because Sarai was the "boss," Hagar had played passive. But when Hagar conceived, she dared to look with disdain upon Sarai who in turn mistreated her until the maid ran away into the wilderness. As Hagar sat weeping near a spring in the desert, not wanting to accept defeat, the angel of the Lord appeared to her and told her to return to her mistress. As a reward for her obedience, God would *so increase* [her] *descendants that they* [would] *be too numerous to count*" (Genesis 16:9–10). She was to name her son *Ishmael,* which means "God hears" when you cry out to Him.

Consulting the Map

The name *Ishmael* means "God hears." Read the following verses to determine what God's Word says about God hearing us when we call out to Him.

Psalm 34:15

_____

1 Peter 3:12

_____

According to these verses, whose prayers does God hear?

_____

Think of a time when God heard your prayers, and write a brief description of that time here.

_____

_____

_____

Hagar replied, *"You are the God who sees me...I have now seen the One who sees me"* (Genesis 16:13). Hagar met God in the wilderness and because she obeyed Him, God made Ishmael the father of the Arab nations.

When patient Abram was ninety-nine years old, the Lord appeared to him again to confirm the covenant. The power of God caused Abram to fall flat on his face in abject humility. As a reward God changed his name to *Abraham,* which means "father of many nations." He also changed Sarai's name to *Sarah,* which means "princess," and reaffirmed that she would have a son. Both Abraham and Sarah laughed at the prospect, and God told them to name their son *Isaac,* which means "laughter."

For Abraham's part of the covenant, he was to be obedient to God. God told him to *"walk before me and be blameless"* (Genesis 17:1). He was also to establish the policy of circumcising each male child who was eight days old (Genesis 17:9–14).

When Abraham, who didn't want to see anyone get hurt, asked God what was to become of Ishmael, He replied, *"I will surely bless him; I will make him fruitful and will greatly increase his numbers. He will be the father of twelve rulers and I will make him into a great nation"* (Genesis 17:20). Today's present-day Arab people are the descendants of Ishmael.

Abraham was 100 years old when his son Isaac was finally born to Sarah. On the eighth day after Isaac's birth, Abraham circumcised his son as God had commanded. Although Sarah had seemed to accept Ishmael before Isaac's birth, as her own Isaac grew up she became angered by Hagar's child, and one day she told Abraham what she wanted him to do: *"Get rid of that slave woman and her son, for that slave woman's son will never share in the inheritance with my son Isaac"* (Genesis 21:10). Isn't it amazing how the thought of sharing an inheritance, both then and today, brings out the baser nature in each one of us?!

Abraham became depressed because he did, in fact, love Ishmael, and so he called out to God who answered him:

> "Do not be so distressed about the boy and your maidservant. Listen to whatever Sarah tells you, because it is through Isaac that your offspring will be reckoned. I will make the son of the maidservant into a nation also, because he is your offspring."
>
> —Genesis 21:12–13

There was no roadmap to the wilderness of the desert:

The next morning Hagar and Ishmael left. *She went on her way and wandered in the desert of Beersheba* (Genesis 21:14). As Hagar sobbed in the wilderness because life was out of her control, God called down from heaven and asked, *"What is the matter, Hagar? Do not be afraid; God has heard the boy crying as he lies there. Lift the boy up and take him by the hand, for I will make him into a great nation"* (Genesis 21:17–18).

When she looked around, Hagar saw a well of water and knew then that God would provide. Ishmael grew up in the wilderness, became an archer, and married an Egyptian. However, it is easy to see why the rejected Ishmael had little fondness for his favored brother, Isaac, and the Hebrew people as a whole. No wonder 4,000 years later the Arabs and the Jews still have an inborn enmity toward each other and cannot live together in peace. Because of the animosity that began with Ishmael and Isaac, the two sides are still fighting and refusing to follow the logical plan for peace.

The roadmap led to the wilderness of Mount Moriah:

As we follow our roadmap back to where these current problems all began, we find that Abraham dearly loved his son Isaac. This boy was his son of promise, and Abraham must have been shocked when God told him to take Isaac up to Mount Moriah and sacrifice him as a burnt offering. But Abraham had pledged obedience to the Lord, and because he loved God so much, he was willing to sacrifice his own son. As he lifted the knife to kill Isaac, who had obediently laid his life on the altar, Abraham heard the voice of God saying, *"Do not lay a hand on the boy.... Do not do anything to him. Now I know that you fear God, because you have not withheld from me your son, your only son"* (Genesis 22:12).

Because Abraham had not withheld his own son, God reaffirmed His pledge to bless the Hebrew race and make them a very special people.

Abraham walked with God, he talked with God, he visited with God, he obeyed God, and because of his close relationship with God, he and his descendants were blessed. Abraham, Sarah, and Hagar all found God in the wilderness.

For Us in Today's World

How many of us feel we are wandering around in a spiritual wilderness? We haven't seen God in months. We wonder if He remembers us. We may have disobeyed a few instructions God made clear to us, and who knows what we've done with those things "on the fringes." We've been a little deceptive here and there, but always for good reason and usually just to save unnecessary confrontation. So why don't we feel close to God? Why are we so lonely in the wilderness?

Elizabeth Dent, a radio personality in Baton Rouge, said to me one day, "I wandered in the Desert of Divorce and I wanted to die." In her time of loneliness, depression, and despair, she, like David, cried out to God.

> *The righteous cry out, and the LORD hears them;*
> *he delivers them from all their troubles.*
> *The LORD is close to the brokenhearted*
> *and saves those who are crushed in spirit.*

> —Psalm 34:17–18

The Lord heard Elizabeth wandering in the wilderness, and they became close in spirit. As she prayed and studied God's Word, He healed her broken heart. During that time of painful growth, Elizabeth wrote poetry to God — as David did in the Psalms. She listened in the darkness so she could give a message to others when she was in the light.

> Lord, thank You for being my Guide each day.
> Thank You for teaching me how to pray.
> You're a special friend, Lord, who's always there.
> Help me give to others what You and I share.[2]

Trip Journal

1. When have you become impatient, as Sarai did, and pushed for something you regretted later?

2. What were the consequences?

3. What conflicts have you experienced with two women trying to function in the same house?

4. How did you solve the problem?

5. Did you send the offending woman to the "desert"?

At the Well and on the Rocks

Read Genesis 24–28.

One of my favorite Bible stories has always been that of Rebekah at the well. Even as a child, I thought how romantic it would be to stand by a well (or even a bus stop) and have some stranger pick me out and change my life forever — whether it was to be the bride of some rich man who lived far away, or to become a Hollywood star, didn't matter. When I heard that Lana Turner, the glamorous movie actress, had been discovered while sitting on a stool at a drugstore soda fountain, I began to practice looking "glamorous" while in pharmacies. Unfortunately, because I had none of Lana's assets, I was never snatched up by any movie producers — or Prince Charming — or even one of the local boys!

Rebekah's story has a much happier ending. Let's forget about our youthful rejections for now, and travel to the town of Nahor where we can see how Rebekah was discovered, chosen by an angel of God.

As we take a look at her love story, her marriage to Isaac, and the birth of her twins, we will see that even a girl handpicked by God can still try to bring life under her own control. Rebekah became deceptive with her husband and passed that trait on to her son Jacob. First Rebekah met Abraham's servant at the well, and then she and Isaac fell in love. Later we will watch Jacob meet God face to face on the rocks.

For God's People in Bible Times

Abraham was growing old, and before he died, he desired to find an appropriate wife for his son Isaac. Abraham called his chief servant before him and instructed him to return to his homeland in northwest Mesopotamia in order to find Isaac a wife. He told the servant that God would send an angel through the wilderness before him and show him which girl should be chosen. The servant did as Abraham instructed, and when he got to the town of Nahor, near Haran, he prayed to God, asking that the right girl for Isaac would give him a drink from the well and then also offer to water his camels.

Before he had finished praying, Rebekah came out with her jar on her shoulder.... The girl was very beautiful, a virgin (Genesis 24:15–16). Rebekah went down to the spring, filled her jar, and came up to where the servant was waiting. When he asked her for a drink, she gave it to him and then volunteered to pour water in the trough for his camels. When he asked her name and family, he was amazed to find that God had chosen the granddaughter of Abraham's brother Nahor. Rebekah took the servant to her home where he explained his mission. Before asking Rebekah's hand in marriage for Isaac, the servant did as we might have done in a similar situation. He not only established the bloodline of Isaac, but he told the prospective in-laws about Isaac's wealth — his sheep, cattle, silver, gold, menservants, maidservants, camels, and donkeys. And after that, he explained how the Lord guided him to Rebekah at the well: *Then the servant brought out gold and silver jewelry and articles of clothing and gave them to Rebekah; he also gave costly gifts to her brother and to her mother* (Genesis 24:53). Gifts to the mother are always a good idea!

Rebekah must have been a daring and self-confident girl to take off with strangers without any fear — or she truly believed God had a plan for her life. The next day when she left with the servant to become Isaac's wife, her brothers gave her a parting blessing: *Our sister, may you increase to thousands upon thousands; may your offspring possess the gates of their enemies* (Genesis 24:60).

The servant and Rebekah had both met God at the well and because they obeyed His plan, He blessed them.

After Sarah's death, Abraham married Keturah. They had at least six other sons whom he sent to other lands, leaving the family flocks and wealth to Isaac. Isaac was forty years old when he married Rebekah, and he was sixty when she became pregnant with twins. These two babies *jostled each other within her,* and she called out to God, *"Why is this happening to me?"* (Genesis 25:22).

The Lord answered Rebekah:

> *"Two nations are in your womb, and two peoples from within you will be separated; one people will be stronger than the other, and the older will serve the younger."*
>
> —Genesis 25:23

The firstborn of the twins was red, and his whole body was covered with hair, and so they named him *Esau,* meaning "hairy." When Esau's brother came out just after him, his hand was clinging to Esau's heel, and so he was named *Jacob,* meaning literally, "he grasps the heel," but figuratively meaning, "he deceives." The twins were so different in both looks and personality that each became a favorite of one of their parents. Gentle Isaac loved Esau, the adventurous hunter, the "outdoorsman" who brought wild game home to his father. Rebekah doted on Jacob, the quieter son who preferred to stay home among the tents.

One day when Esau came charging home, famished from hunting, Jacob had some red stew and hot bread prepared. It was then that Jacob saw his chance to gain control over his older twin. Before he would give his starving brother food, he made Esau promise to sell him his birthright. Without giving any real thought to the future and wishing to satisfy the physical needs of the moment, Esau agreed and sold his birthright for a dish of stew.

While this agreement may appear extremely shortsighted to us, we could each think of some time in our lives when we made a rash decision based on expediency or the pleasures of the moment, without analyzing the needs of our future or the possible repercussions of our actions.

Consulting the Map

While in our culture, parents work very hard to treat all their children equally, in biblical times, the "birthright" was very important.

Read the following verses and note what is important about the recipient of the birthright's position and property:

Position: Genesis 49

_____

Property: Deuteronomy 21:15–17

_____

Read the following verses to understand how these same attributes applied to the nation of Israel.

_____

Exodus 4:22

_____

Jeremiah 31:9

_____

Psalm 89:27

_____

The term *birthright* is only mentioned once in the New Testament. Read Hebrews 12:16. To what, or to whom, is the term *birthright* referring?

_____

We can clearly see that the birthright was typically given to the oldest son, the firstborn. How does this understanding of these Old Testament references help us to better understand Christ and His role in our life?

_____

_____

Read the following verses and note Jesus Christ's position over us.

Position: Colossians 1:15

_____

Property: Hebrews 1:6

_____

Read Galatians 3:26 and Hebrews 1:6. As Christians, we are the _____ of God. If Christ is the firstborn Son of God, we are His _____. Because He is the firstborn, and we are the siblings, we must give Him authority in our lives.

At this time, a famine came to the land, and Isaac considered moving his family to Egypt in order to find food. But then the Lord appeared to him and said, _"Do not go down to Egypt; live in the land where I tell you to live. Stay in this land for a while, and I will be with you and will bless you"_ (Genesis 26:2–3). God then reviewed the covenant He had made with Isaac's father, Abraham, promising to make Isaac's descendants as plentiful as the stars in the sky if he would obey God's commands. So agreeable Isaac stayed in Gerar, present-day Gaza, and the Lord blessed him: *The man became rich, and his wealth continued to grow until he became very wealthy* (verse 13).

How God delights in blessing those who are obedient to His will!

When Isaac grew old, his eyesight failed, and he knew that he would soon die. He called for his favorite and eldest son, Esau, to come to him in order to pass on his birthright and inheritance and give him the official family blessing. First, he asked Esau to go hunting and then prepare him his favorite dish. As soon as Esau left, Rebekah, who had been eavesdropping on her husband's conversation with their firstborn son, called her favorite son, Jacob, and told him of the deceptive plan she had schemed. Not only was Jacob her favorite son, but she did not want Esau to get the blessing and inheritance because she couldn't stand Esau's wives. In her own controlling and independent way — which had served her well from her youth — she declared, *"I'm disgusted with living because of these Hittite women"* (Genesis 27:46). Esau's wives, in Rebekah's mind, were obviously from the wrong side of the tracks, and they were driving her crazy: *"If Jacob takes a wife from among the women of this land, from Hittite women like these, my life will not be worth living,"* she said (verse 46).

After considering her love for Jacob, and her disgust of Esau's wives, Rebekah, who had once met God at the well herself, rationalized that even God would understand her deceptive ploy. She prepared food for Isaac, put Esau's clothes on Jacob, and put goatskins on his arms so he would seem hairy like Esau was. When Jacob questioned her plan, saying, *"I would appear to be tricking him and would bring down a curse on myself rather than a blessing,"* Rebekah answered, *"My son, let the curse fall on me. Just do what I say"* (Genesis 27:12–13).

How many of us have ever put our children up to doing something that we couldn't do ourselves — something even they knew better than to do — and when they were reticent, said as Rebekah did, "Just do what I say!"

Jacob did as she said and deceived his father. And when Isaac asked him directly, *"Are you really my son Esau?"* (verse 24), Jacob lied and then received the rightful blessing of his brother. When Esau returned home from hunting, he went in to see his father and ask for his blessing. Isaac wept when he found out what had happened, and Esau angrily retorted, *"Isn't he rightly named Jacob? He has deceived me these two times: He took my birthright, and now he's taken my blessing!"* (verse 36).

When Esau lost the blessing, he was devastated. In fact, when he discovered that Jacob had stolen it from him, Esau cried out, *"Do you have only one blessing, my father? Bless me too, my father!"* (Genesis 27:38). But in biblical times, once the final blessing from a father was spoken, it was irrevocable. In response to his pitiful cries, Esau did receive a blessing of sorts from his father (see Genesis 27:39–40), but it was not the words of value and acceptance that he had longed to hear.

Can you hear the anguish in Esau's cry, *"Bless me, even me also, O my father"* (KJV)? This same painful cry and unfulfilled longing is echoed today by many people who are searching for their family's blessing, men and women whose parents, for whatever reason, have failed to bless them with words of love and acceptance.

Esau was angry and consoled himself by dwelling on thoughts of murder. He plotted to kill his brother the minute their father died. When Rebekah heard of Esau's plan, she sent Jacob off to live with her brother Laban, in Haran, giving the explanation to Isaac that Jacob must not marry a Hittite woman as Esau had done.

Isaac, accepting his wife's reasoning, gave Jacob the final family blessing. Isaac passed down to Jacob the blessing that God had given to Abraham:

> *"May God Almighty bless you and make you fruitful and increase your numbers until you become a community of peoples. May he give you and your descendants the blessing given to Abraham, so that you may take possession of the land where you now live as an alien, the land God gave to Abraham."*
>
> —Genesis 28:3–4

How often God's covenant with Abraham is reviewed in the Old Testament — and how alive it is today as Israel constantly scraps to possess and preserve the land God promised them through Abraham, Isaac, and Jacob!

On his way to Haran, Jacob, who just days before had had no thought of leaving home, stopped for the night out in the wilderness. He took a rock from a pile and used it for a pillow. (That may not sound very comfortable, but I've slept in motels where I'm sure they got the pillows from that same pile. No wonder Jacob had dreams!) In his dream, Jacob saw a ladder that reached up to God in heaven. Angels were going up and down the ladder, and then God spoke to him and said:

> *"I am the LORD, the God of your father Abraham and the God of Isaac. I will give you and your descendants the land on which you are lying. Your descendants will be like the dust of the earth, and you will spread out to the west and to the east, to the north and to the south. All peoples on earth will be blessed through you and your offspring. I am with you and will watch over you wherever you go, and I will bring you back to this land. I will not leave you until I have done what I have promised you."*
>
> —Genesis 28:13–15

When Jacob awoke, he marveled at God's goodness to him in spite of his deceptive acts:

> *"Surely the LORD is in this place, and I was not aware of it.... How awesome is this place! This is none other than the house of God; this is the gate of heaven."*
>
> —Genesis 28:16–17

Jacob made the stone he had slept on into a monument to God and pledged him one-tenth of his future income. He named the place *Bethel*, meaning "house of God," and pledged that if God would bring him home safely and provide for his basic needs, he would choose Him as his God forever. Jacob was never the same after he met God face to face on the rocks.

Consulting the Map

Read Genesis 28:22.

Jacob's experience with God on the rocks was what we might call a rededication of his life to God, as he promised to choose Him as his God. According to Genesis 28:22, what was the physical manifestation of Jacob's dedication to God?

_____

_____

Read Genesis 14:20.

_____

Was Jacob's gift to God a new idea?

_____

_____

Read each of the following verses. How much is given to God in these passages? Because God is an intangible being, how are the gifts given to God?

	PORTION	GIVEN TO WHOM
Numbers 18:21	_____	_____
Deuteronomy 26:12	_____	_____
Nehemiah 12:44	_____	_____

How can these lessons apply to your life today?

_____

_____

Read Proverbs 3:9.

According to this verse, what does our giving show about our relationship with God?

_____

_____

Write a prayer asking God to help you honor Him with your gifts to the church leadership and to those in need.

_____

_____

_____

_____

For Us in Today's World

How often we say "the whole thing's on the rocks. It's over. There's no hope." Are you feeling "on the rocks" today? Look up to God as Jacob did in his wilderness, for wherever you are, this spot may be your gate to heaven.

A dear lady named Jill, who had gone through an unwanted and humiliating divorce, wrote me that she and her children had been "on the rocks." In fact she said that she couldn't "find a rock big enough to hide under or a place on this earth far enough away to stop the pain." She had done all she knew to do to save her marriage, but her husband had left her for a secretary in his office. "She needed a daddy for her daughter, and she got ours!"

What do you do when you're left alone on the rocks? Jill cried out to God to fill the aching void in her life, and He met her in her wilderness.

Consulting the Map

God was with Jacob even through his sin and wanderings in the wilderness. As we learned in Lesson 7, God was with Abraham in the wilderness. And God was with Jill in her rocky wilderness experience.

Read Joshua 1:5.
What does this verse tell you about God's presence with you when it seems that your life is "on the rocks"?

_____

_____

In the following space, journal about a time when it seemed that everyone was against you, but ultimately you saw that God was with you.

_____

_____

_____

_____

_____

_____

_____

_____

How did this experience on life's rocky road prepare you for future trials?

_____

_____

_____

_____

Sometimes we have to get between a rock and a hard place to look sincerely for our God, but like Jacob, we, too, can meet God on the rocks.

Trip Journal

1. Abraham is considered a "type" of God the Father and his son Isaac is a "type" of Christ. A "type" is a prophetic representation, one thing pre-figuring another. A "symbol" is a representation, one thing standing for another. What similarities do you see to support this theory?

2. If your parents had chosen a mate for you at the well, who would it have been and why? Did they talk about what kind of person you should marry? What traits did they want to see in your spouse?

3. What personality traits do you see running through Abraham's family? Through your own family? Through your mate's family? What are you passing on to your children?

4. What is the difference between the birthright and the blessing? How do you feel your parents either gave or withheld the blessing of acceptance and approval? How are you blessing your own children?

5. Can you say of your time on the rocks, as Jacob did, *"Surely the LORD is in this place.... This is the gate of heaven"*?

6. For additional reading on the topic of the family blessing, see *The Blessing* by Gary Smalley and John Trent (Thomas Nelson, 1986).

Scenic Overlook

About forty years ago, when I was a new-believing Christian and just starting to give my testimony, I was asked to speak at a retreat near Mount Shasta. When I arrived, I discovered, to my dismay, that the campgrounds and cabins were very "rustic" — meaning that they had few amenities. Since my idea of "camping out" is opening the window in my room at the Holiday Inn, I was far from delighted over the circumstances. I soon learned that my opening message was to be given outdoors, in the dark, by a campfire. It had never occurred to me that I wouldn't be speaking in some kind of a building with at least some flicker of light, but instead, I found myself out in a field, sitting on a rock. A few bright flames, fanned by the breeze, passed flickering shadows over the faces of my audience, as the campfire lit up their eyes and the moon reflected off the top of Mount Shasta. The scene had quite a friendly glow — that is, until the mosquitoes came out and began to buzz in our ears, the moon went behind the clouds, the rocks grew harder and harder, the fire died out, and the night chill crept inside our sweaters.

Some voice out of the dark introduced me, and I gave my testimony to what might have been no one — I didn't know, because at first I couldn't see at all. Occasionally the moon would peek out long enough for me to see silhouettes and know there was an audience in the shadows.

At the end, I offered up a prayer of commitment, asking those who had not yet found God in a personal way to ask Jesus Christ into their lives. There was no apparent response.

Years passed, and as I began to speak in bigger and brighter places, I forgot that humbling evening on the rocks. Eighteen years later I was speaking at a large retreat for women in an elegant hotel when a lovely lady approached me. "Do you remember sharing your testimony at Mount Shasta State Park?" she asked. An instant recall zipped into my mind, and I was about to share a laugh with her over the "bad old days," when I noticed the serious look on her face and the moistening in her eyes. "It was that night in the dark that I prayed with you to receive Christ. I'd been looking for God, but I'd never seen Him in the light. Somehow the protection of darkness gave me courage, and I dared to ask Jesus into my life without letting anyone know." She then filled me in on the changes in her life that had taken place since that night, including a successful marriage to a Christian leader.

"Thank you for being willing to come to the State Park and speak. Your obedience to God changed the direction of my life," she told me.

How unworthy of her praise I felt as I remembered my attitude that night, for while I had felt a surge of self-pity for my situation, she had found God on the rocks.

LESSON 9

In a Foreign Land

Read Genesis 29–39.

With the ease of air travel today, many of us look forward to visiting a foreign land someday to experience another culture and place. For Jacob, however, his travels weren't easy as he wandered through the wilderness in the direction of Haran, hoping to find a wife. How often we think there would be romance if only we were in some castle on the Rhine, lying on the sands of the Riviera, or waltzing to "The Blue Danube" in Vienna. Let's follow Jacob as he finds love among the sheep, and more wives than he bargained for.

For God's People in Bible Times

After Jacob found God on the rocks, he continued on to Haran — his mother's homeland but a foreign place to him. Just as Jacob's mother had been discovered at the well, it was also at a well that Jacob spotted the beautiful Rachel, his cousin, as she came to water her father's sheep. He fell in love with her at first sight and rolled away the stone from the well for her as if it were a pebble. As her sheep drank, Jacob identified himself. He kissed his cousin and was so overwhelmed that he cried out loud. But as captivating as Rachel was, the opposite seemed true of her sister, Leah, who is sometimes described as "wall-eyed." Whether this means that each eye faced a different wall, I don't know, but it is clear that today she would have "faded into the wallpaper" when compared with Rachel, who was *lovely in form* (Genesis 29:17).

Jacob's complete fascination with Rachel, who could easily have been a candidate for the Miss Haran crown, caused him to pledge to his uncle to work seven years with no wages in order to marry Rachel. Can you imagine such dedication? *But they seemed like only a few days to him because of his love for her* (Genesis 29:20).

We know that Rachel was well chaperoned during this time and Jacob's love was from a distance, for at the end of the seven years he asked Laban for Rachel's hand in marriage. *"Give me my wife. My time is completed, and I want to lie with her"* (Genesis 29:21).

Laban put on a great feast and invited everyone he knew to the wedding. Jacob went to this celebration feast and then spent the night with his bride. But when morning came and he opened his eyes, there was Leah — not Rachel! He'd been deceived by his father-in-law. Isn't it amazing how God allows us to reap what we have sown? Jacob had deceived his brother and his father, and now it was his turn to be on the receiving end.

When Jacob complained in anger to Laban, his uncle replied that it was not the custom to marry the younger daughter off before the older, and he was therefore justified in substituting Leah as the bride. *"Finish this daughter's bridal week; then we will give you the younger one also, in return for another seven years of work"* was Laban's final verdict (Genesis 29:27).

Jacob had little choice, so he kept Leah as his wife, received Rachel at the end of the week, and then had to work for free for another seven years! Let's hope it again seemed as only a few days because he loved Rachel so much.

Although Leah was neither beautiful nor loved by her husband, she was fertile, and she produced Jacob's first son, *Reuben,* whose name means, "See, a son!" and in the Hebrew sounded like the words, "For God has seen my misery." Since this birth gave Leah an edge over Rachel, she wanted to increase her advantage. She conceived again and produced *Simeon,* whose name means "one who hears": *"Because the LORD heard that I am not loved, he gave me this one too,"* Leah explained (verse 33).

Leah hoped Jacob would finally become more attached to her than he was to childless Rachel, so she named her third son *Levi,* which means "attached." When the fourth son came along, she praised the Lord and named him *Judah,* which means "praise."

Rachel was still at zero in this child-bearing contest, and she cried out to Jacob, *"Give me children, or I'll die!"* (Genesis 30:1). Jacob attested that he was sure it wasn't his fault, and so she insisted he have a child by her maid, Bilhah. How like Sarah, Jacob's grandmother, who hadn't believed God could produce children by her in her old age and who sent her husband into her maid, thus producing Ishmael, the father of the Arab races.

When Bilhah conceived, Rachel was relieved. This was a son for "her side," even though he did not come from her own body. She named this child *Dan*, which means, "He has vindicated," and then suggested another try. The next son born in this great contest was called *Naphtali*, "my struggle."

Leah, not to be outdone, offered up her maid, Zilpah, who then produced *Gad*, meaning "What good fortune!" This birth made Leah so happy that she sent Jacob into her maid again and named the next son *Asher*, which means "happiness." Leah also called out to God to give her another son from her own body, and the Lord answered. Her fifth son she named *Issachar*, which means "my reward," and he was soon followed by a sixth. Leah knew that Jacob would finally have to "honor" her as the winner, so Leah named this child *Zebulun*, which means "my honor."

Poor Rachel had given up by now and had confessed to God her disgrace as a barren woman. Isn't it amazing how when we give up striving for what we want and begin to accept our situation, God rewards us! Miraculously, Rachel became pregnant and gave birth to her first son. She took that event to be a new beginning for her and named her child *Joseph*, which means, "May God add another."

Once Jacob finally had a son by his beloved Rachel, he began to think of that boy's future — despite all of the other sons he had. Although Laban had deceived and cheated Jacob, Jacob's flocks had still been the ones to multiply, and this infuriated his father-in-law. When Jacob wondered what to do about the situation, God told him clearly, *"Now leave this land at once and go back to your native land"* (Genesis 31:13).

Jacob gathered together his family, flocks, and possessions and left for home without telling Laban. When Laban heard of this deception, he pursued Jacob and found him and his whole family camped in the hill country of Gilead.

Laban called out to Jacob:

> *"What have you done? You've deceived me, and you've carried off my daughters like captives in war. Why did you run off secretly and deceive me? Why didn't you tell me, so I could send you away with joy and singing to the music of tambourines and harps?"*
>
> —Genesis 31:26–27

Laban gave the impression that he would have thrown a festive farewell party, even though nothing in his past behavior would suggest this possibility.

Jacob answered, *"I was afraid"* (verse 31).

Isn't that the reason we have used for our deception? "I was afraid." Little children lie when they are caught in disobedience because they're afraid of the punishment. As adults, many of us tell little white lies to escape blame. Some of us pretend to be what we aren't because we are afraid that if anyone knew the real person behind our mask, they wouldn't like us. Jacob was just like we and our children are: He was afraid that if he told Laban where he was really going, Laban wouldn't let him go. So fear caused him to deceive Laban, even though God had promised to be with Jacob as he returned to the land of his fathers.

Consulting the Map

As we can see, fear caused Jacob to make poor choices that resulted in lying and deception. Let's look at what God's Word has to say about fear. Many verses in the Bible tell us to "fear not," and yet many others say that we should fear certain things.

Read the following passages and note if they say to "fear not" or to "fear," and why. (Hint: Reading several translations may be helpful to you in this exercise.)

	"FEAR NOT" OR "FEAR"?	WHY?
Deuteronomy 31:6	_____	_____
1 Samuel 12:20	_____	_____
2 Kings 6:16	_____	_____
2 Chronicles 19:7	_____	_____
Proverbs 29:25	_____	_____
Matthew 10:28	_____	_____
2 Timothy 1:7	_____	_____
1 Peter 1:17	_____	_____

Based on what you have learned from these verses, do you think Jacob was right in being afraid? Why or why not?

_____

_____

What is the common theme you find with the words, *Fear not*?

_____

_____

With the word *fear*?

_____

_____

Jacob couldn't accept God's plan for him without taking matters into his own hands and even skirting the truth when necessary. Any time we are not doing what we know God wants of us and we are afraid of being caught, we have the human urge to lie. Disobedience breeds deception, and deception ran in Jacob's family:

1. Abraham deceived both the Pharaoh of Egypt and King Abimelech of Gerar by saying his wife was his sister. He was afraid of the consequences of telling the truth (Genesis 12:11–20; 20:2–18).

2. Isaac deceived King Abimelech in the same way for the same reason: *"Because I thought I might lose my life on account of her"* (Genesis 26:6–16).

3. Rebekah deceived her husband into giving the blessing to the wrong son (Genesis 27:1–29).

4. Jacob went along with his mother and deceived his elderly father (Genesis 27:18–29).

5. Jacob deceived his brother, Esau, twice, taking Esau's birthright and blessing (Genesis 27:36).

6. Rebekah deceived Isaac again by pretending to send Jacob away to get a wife when she actually feared that Esau would kill him (Genesis 27:42–46).

7. Laban deceived Jacob into marrying Leah (Genesis 29:22–28).

8. Jacob and Laban deceived each other about their flocks and wages (Genesis 30:25–31:9).

Finally, the two deceptive men, Jacob and Laban, faced each other and their past behavior. They agreed to be honest with each other and to call a truce. Out in the hill country of Gilead, they pledged to the God of Abraham and made a covenant of peace between them.

Jacob set a stone up as a pillar, and the relatives piled rocks around it in a heap. They called the monument *Galeed,* or "witness heap," and because neither one really trusted the other, they called the place *Mizpah,* which means "watchtower."

As they put up the final stone, Laban called upon God, the only Person he knew who actually was honest: *"The LORD watch between me and thee, when we are absent one from another"* (Genesis 31:49, KJV).

Consulting the Map

Both Jacob and Laban were dishonest with each other. Read Proverbs 11:3 and 12:22. What do these verses say about honesty?

_____

_____

About dishonesty?

_____

_____

For Us in Today's World

Each time I read Genesis 31:49 in its proper context — that of two untrusting men asking God to keep watch over the other — I am amused at recalling the use of that verse in my childhood. Our minister always recited it as his benediction, so I grew up thinking it was a nice way to end a service, a pleasant farewell to the congregation: *"May the LORD keep watch between you and me when we are away from each other."*

Until I began to study Genesis, I never realized that the true impact of this verse came only with an understanding of the story of Laban and Jacob — when we can't trust each other, we ask God to be our watchtower. How important it is to study verses within their context.

How about your family? Does deception run in your bloodline? Are there some who tell lies as smoothly as they tell the truth? Are there some for whom "deception" is their middle name?

In Psalm 101:7, God declares: *"No one who practices deceit will dwell in my house; no one who speaks falsely will stand in my presence."* And in Proverbs 12:22, we learn, *The LORD detests lying lips, but he delights in men who are truthful.*

If we wish to find God in our "foreign lands," we must acknowledge that He delights in people who are truthful. Maybe we need to pile up some rocks as a monument to truthfulness, name it *Galeed* — "witness heap" — and ask God to watch over our tongues to keep them honest. God wants to meet us wherever we are, but no one who speaks falsely will stand in His presence.

For God's People in Bible Times

As we pick up our story of Jacob the deceiver, we find that after he took an oath of honesty before God and his father-in-law, he invited his relatives to a meal. The next day, Laban returned home, and Jacob went on his way toward Edom and his brother, Esau, who years ago had vowed to kill him. Jacob sent messengers ahead to let Esau know he was on his way home. When the messengers returned saying that Esau was coming to meet him with 400 men, the same fear that had first caused Jacob to flee to Haran gripped him again. He divided his wives, children, and flocks into two groups so that if Esau attacked one side, the others could escape. He also sent servants ahead with gifts in the hopes of appeasing his brother: 200 female goats, 20 male goats, 200 ewes, 20 rams, 30 female camels, 40 cows, 10 bulls, 20 female donkeys, and 10 males. Hardly what we'd expect to find under our Christmas tree, and certainly more than we could keep in our own backyards!

Jacob thought to himself, *I will pacify him with these gifts I am sending on ahead; later, when I see him, perhaps he will receive me* (Genesis 32:20).

As Jacob lay alone that night in the wilderness, far away from home, across the stream from where he had placed his family, a mysterious man came to him and tried to wrestle him to the ground. Jacob fought with him until daybreak, and when the man found he couldn't hold Jacob down, he touched the socket of Jacob's hip and wrenched it. The man asked Jacob for his name, and when Jacob told him, the man said, *"Your name will no longer be Jacob, but Israel* [he struggles with God], *because you have struggled with God and with men and have overcome"* (verse 28). The man then blessed him, and Jacob named the place *Peniel*, which means, "I saw God face to face" (verse 30).

God was gracious to Jacob and caused Esau, the founder of Edom, the "land of red earth," to welcome him back home after his many years in a foreign land. The prophecy that God had given Rebekah before her sons' birth had been fulfilled:

"Two nations are in your womb, and two peoples from within you will be separated; one people will be stronger than the other, and the older will serve the younger."

—Genesis 25:23

God instructed Jacob to settle near Bethel in the land of Canaan and to build an altar on the very spot where God had revealed himself to Jacob when he was fleeing from his brother. Before going to Bethel to build the altar, Jacob buried all the foreign gods and statues that his family had brought with them. Later, God spoke to Jacob by the altar he had built and gave him a promise:

"I am God Almighty; be fruitful and increase in number. A nation and a community of nations will come from you, and kings will come from your body. The land I gave to Abraham and Isaac I also give to you, and I will give this land to your descendants after you."

—Genesis 35:11–12

The promise God had given to Abraham in his childless old age — the promise that seemed so remote and impossible at the time — was on its way to fulfillment. But before the caravan reached their home, Rachel went into labor with her second son and died in childbirth. Just before her death, she named him *Ben-Oni,* which means "son of my trouble," but after she died, Jacob renamed his baby, *Benjamin,* which means "son of my right hand." Jacob buried his beloved Rachel near Bethlehem and made a stone pillar to commemorate her grave.

By the time Joseph grew to be a young man, his father, Jacob, had established himself in Canaan with his family and was prospering in the land that God had promised his grandfather Abraham.

Joseph was a precocious and gifted child and was clearly his father's favorite son, born in Jacob's old age to the beautiful Rachel. To show his special love for Joseph, Jacob gave him a one-of-a-kind coat of many colors, richly ornamented: *"When his brothers saw that their father loved him more than any of them, they hated him and could not speak a kind word to him"* (Genesis 37:4).

How sad it is and yet how true to human nature that petty jealousy so often splits families. It's the same today as it was in the time of Joseph: If one brother turns out to be smarter, richer, or more talented, often those brothers less fortunate than he turn against him and talk behind his back.

Consulting the Map

It is easy to point a finger at Joseph's brothers when we see how their jealousy brought great harm to their brother's life. Because most of us do not have that degree of jealousy, we do not often pay attention to the jealous feelings that we do have.

Read the following verses. What does each of them say about the condition of your spiritual life when jealousy is present?

Romans 13:13

_____

1 Corinthians 3:3

_____

Galatians 5:19–26

_____

James 3:15–16

_____

From the above verses, we can see that jealousy is the result of our spiritual condition. If there is jealousy in your heart, stop now and write out a prayer asking God to replace the sin of jealousy with the fruit of His Spirit.

_____

_____

_____

Joseph had the natural traits of a powerful personality. He was what would be termed today a "gifted" child, and he was too young to realize that his open expression and excitement about his abilities would make his brothers feel inconsequential in comparison. As he matured and became closer to God, his brashness was buffered and his leadership qualities ultimately became useful.

Joseph had the additional God-given gift of interpreting dreams, which further alienated him from his peers. Worse than having this talent was the fact that every dream he had showed him to be important and his brothers to be insignificant. Had Joseph realized the deep-seated hostility his brothers had for him, he might have been wise enough not to share his dreams with them, but being secure in his father's love and excited about his unusual talent, he wanted to let everyone know what he had dreamed.

Joseph made the mistake of telling his brothers about one of his dreams in which they were binding sheaves of grain out in the fields. Suddenly, his sheaf stood upright while his brothers' sheaves bowed down before his in humility. You can imagine how well this idea went over with his brothers who were already jealous. The mere thought that they would ever have to bow down to the younger Joseph in his gaudy coat infuriated them all. They must have hidden their wrath well, or perhaps Joseph was so full of excitement that he didn't notice, because he later told them of his next dream: *"Listen," he said, "I had another dream, and this time the sun and moon and eleven stars were bowing down to me"* (Genesis 37:9).

That was more than Joseph's brothers could handle. No doubt at least one of them mumbled, "If I ever get my hands on the kid, I'll kill him." And eventually they did get their hands on Joseph. One day as the brothers were out in the wilderness allowing their sheep to graze, Jacob sent Joseph to check on them:

> *So Joseph went after his brothers and found them near Dothan. But they saw him in the distance, and before he reached them, they plotted to kill him.*
> —Genesis 37:17–18

Finally, here was their great opportunity to get rid of this spoiled teenage brother who was constantly irking them with his visions of grandeur. As Joseph approached — wearing his expensive coat, as usual — the brothers decided to unite against him and exact punishment far greater than Joseph's innocent pride deserved.

"Here comes that dreamer!" they said to each other. "Come now, let's kill him and throw him into one of these cisterns and say that a ferocious animal devoured him. Then we'll see what comes of his dreams."

—Genesis 37:19–20

Reuben, the oldest, had a slight twinge of conscience and suggested that they simply throw him into the empty well without killing him. So that's what they did, and with little emotion or remorse, they all sat down nearby to eat their meal in peace. As they ate their food, they saw a band of Ishmaelites passing by on their way to Egypt, their camels loaded down with spices, balm, and myrrh. These men had to be descendants of their grandfather's half-brother, Ishmael, and therefore relatives from the "wrong side of the family."

When Judah saw this caravan, he said to his brothers:

"What will we gain if we kill our brother and cover up his blood? Come, let's sell him to the Ishmaelites and not lay our hands on him; after all, he is our brother, our own flesh and blood."

—Genesis 37:26–27

Noble Judah! The brothers pulled Joseph out of the cistern and sold him for twenty shekels of silver, about sixty-four dollars in today's market.

To cover up their deed, they took the hated coat, smeared it with the blood of a goat, and carried it to their father's tent. When they showed it to him and asked if he thought it could be Joseph's, the poor distraught man cried out, *"It is my son's robe! Some ferocious animal has devoured him. Joseph has surely been torn to pieces"* (Genesis 37:33).

The brothers tried to comfort their father, but he vowed to mourn Joseph to his grave. Notice that the brothers didn't actually *lie,* per se; they were just following the family pattern of deception that had been passed down through Abraham, Isaac, and Jacob. They allowed their father to make a faulty conclusion, relieving them somewhat of their guilt.

For Us in Today's World

How relieved we sometimes feel when people jump to the wrong conclusion without our having to lie about the situation!

There is no evidence that Joseph's brothers had ever had a personal experience with God, but the Bible tells us that Joseph surely had. Despite being rejected by his brothers, sold for a handful of silver, and bought by an Egyptian official named Potiphar, Joseph kept his eyes on the Lord. From being taken from a home in which he had servants to being sold as a slave himself, Joseph had every reason to be depressed; yet he knew God was with him — even in Egypt. He refused to let his circumstances get him down, and as he trusted his Lord in these adverse situations, the Lord blessed him and even caused him to prosper.

What a lesson for those of us in financial difficulties or those of us who have been rejected and are without family support. Joseph didn't waste time on self-pity, wondering how a terrible thing like this could happen to a good person like himself. Instead, he drew on his personal strengths and his spiritual reservoir; he got down to the work at hand and thanked the Lord that he was even alive. And the rewards came:

> *When his master saw that the* LORD *was with him and that the* LORD *gave him success in everything he did, Joseph found favor in his eyes and became his attendant. Potiphar put him in charge of his household, and he entrusted to his care everything he owned.*
>
> —Genesis 39:3–4

What have we learned as we've traveled with Joseph to Egypt? Have we been walking so close to the Lord that people who have seen us in the desert know we've been with Jesus? When life has dried up and we have been rejected, have we been able to praise God anyhow? Think of Joseph — what an example he was! Even sold as a slave, he was so close to the Lord that people noticed there was something different about him. Instead of being jealous of Joseph's exceptional spirituality, Potiphar was grateful and left all decisions in Joseph's hands, *except the food he ate* (Genesis 39:6).

Joseph found that God could even be found in Egypt, a pagan country with golden idols. But Satan was also there, that wily serpent who is always on the prowl to catch believers in some moment of weakness. Potiphar's wife had observed how well-built the handsome Joseph was, and she set out to have an affair with him. While we might be tempted to think that aggressive women are a phenomenon of our modern day and age, we have only to listen to Potiphar's wife to know that they've been around forever: *"Come to bed with me!"* she said clearly to Joseph (verse 7). What a tempting opportunity that must have seemed to be — to be seduced by the boss's wife! How many godly men have given in to such a taste of forbidden fruit?

But Joseph knew God, even in Egypt, and he refused to be tempted. He flatly turned her down, explaining that her husband had put him in charge of everything but her, and that he would not violate that trust.

Consulting the Map

Like Joseph, all of us are tempted at one time or another. It may not be the boss's wife, it may be the boss himself — promising favors in exchange for "favors." Or it may be something much more tame, like going where we do not belong or spending money we know we should not spend.

According to 1 Corinthians 10:13, who faces temptation?

_____

Read the following verses and then note the source of temptation found in each.

Matthew 6:13

_____

Luke 4:13

_____

James 1:13–14

_____

When we are tempted, as Scripture says we will be, what do the following verses present as the solution?

Matthew 26:41

_____

Ephesians 6:16

_____

1 Peter 5:9

_____

Poets throughout the centuries have written of the appetites of unrequited love, and we all know that "hell hath no fury like a woman scorned." After repeated invitations, all of which Joseph refused, Potiphar's wife gave one more impassioned plea for attention. As Joseph turned quickly to get out of her sight, she made a desperate grab at his coat, hoping to pull him toward her, not willing to admit that she had been unsuccessful in her bid for love and attention. He fled the temptation, but she was left with his coat in her hands, a limp souvenir of unfulfilled lust. What an insult that she, the lady of the house, would offer herself to a common slave and be turned down! She would show him that he couldn't treat her that way. She called for her servants and displayed to them the proof that Joseph had come to molest her and had fled when she screamed. All afternoon she held the coat close to her, and when her husband came home she lied convincingly, _"That Hebrew slave you brought us came to me to make sport of me. But as soon as I screamed for help, he left his cloak beside me and ran out of the house"_ (Genesis 39:17–18). Believing his wife's report and not taking time to investigate the other side, Potiphar threw Joseph into prison.

Trip Journal

Read Genesis 29–39, paying special note to any examples you see of deception and rejection.

1. Jacob first deceived his father and his brother, and then his father-in-law, Laban, tricked him into marrying Leah when he had worked seven years for Rachel. How did Laban rationalize his actions? Have you ever been deceived or "done in" by a friend or relative? What was the situation and how did you react? What has been, or could be, a healthy resolution of your conflict?

2. Do you have a child who has a pattern of lying? Have you probed his underlying reasons? What would God have you do about this situation? Don't let deception become a family trait.

3. Throughout Scripture, the names of people and places have special meaning, and nowhere is this more noticeable than in the twelve children of Jacob. Review their names and make a list of words and their meanings for your notebook. As we continue our study, there will be other names to add to this list.

4. Although Jacob had met God on the rocks, there were times when he showed a lack of faith in God. He was afraid to face his father-in-law and tell him he was leaving, and he was so fearful about meeting his brother that he divided his family for protection. In what ways are you fearful? Do you recognize fear and worry as a lack of faith in God's plan for your life?

5. Jacob wrestled with God in the night. What wakes you up at night? What struggles do you have when you should be sleeping? What can you do about these concerns? If you had to bury your idols as Jacob did, what would they be?

6. Why was Joseph Jacob's favorite son? Do you have one child who is your favorite? What problems does this cause? What problems did this cause with Joseph's brothers? In retrospect, had Joseph been more mature, what could he have done differently in his sibling relationships?

7. Is there a "wrong side" in your family? A poor group? Some snobs? Phonies? Cheats? Is this really the truth or just a family myth? Are you depriving your children of an acquaintance with some colorful characters or cousins? As a child, I couldn't associate with my father's family because they were of an unacceptable religion. Where do these biases originate, and what can we do to change family attitudes?

8. Joseph was sold as a slave and had every right to be depressed and feel rejected. What reasons from your past do you have for negative feelings? What kept Joseph above his circumstances? What could help you?

9. How did Joseph — an innocent, God-fearing man — get himself into trouble? When did you last take a chance that could have had serious consequences? What lesson can you teach your children from the story of Joseph? How "spiritual" would you be if you were unjustly thrown in prison?

For Your Notebook

Find out the meaning of your name. *Florence* means "blooming flower." *Frederick* means "peaceful ruler." In our family, I've been blooming while Fred's been quietly ruling! Christian bookstores carry plaques with almost every name imaginable, along with their meanings. Why not find one for each member of your family and tie this action in with your study?

Add these names to your list of Bible names, places, and their meanings, and then begin a new record of numbers and their significance below.

For starters, the number *seven* stands for perfection and completeness:

- Noah waited *seven* days each time the dove returned before sending it out of the ark again.
- Jacob worked *seven* years for Leah and *seven* years for Rachel.
- Laban pursued Jacob for *seven* days.
- Jacob bowed down to the ground *seven* times as he approached Esau.

LESSON 10

From Prison to Power

Read Genesis 40–50.

In our last lesson, we left Joseph locked away in prison for something he hadn't done. If we were in Joseph's position, wouldn't most of us be ready to give up on God? From a human perspective, it doesn't make any sense. Joseph was imprisoned — for doing the right thing? If anybody ever had a reason for a pity party, it was him.

Let's face it. Haven't we cried out to God in far less harrowing situations? Haven't we given up when we couldn't see God acting on our behalf — right now? *Lord, You know I'm a good girl. I pray each day and teach a Bible study. Why is this happening to me? Surely You have abandoned me! Oh, woe is me!*

But that wasn't Joseph's response to his harsh, yet totally undeserved, treatment at the hands of a man he had served faithfully and well. Instead he maintained a good attitude. He may have even prayed, *I don't understand, Lord, but if You've allowed me to be here, there must be some reason, so I'll make the best of it and hope someday to see some good in this bad situation.* How unlike most of us!

Joseph was in the pit once again, but because the Lord was with him, Joseph was soon put in charge of the whole prison and all its inmates: *The warden paid no attention to anything under Joseph's care, because the LORD was with Joseph and gave him success in whatever he did* (Genesis 39:23).

As you observe Joseph's behavior, you might ask yourself, "Where am I with the Lord today?" Are you imprisoned in some way? Does some painful situation have a grip on you? Joseph walked with God — even in jail — and he had success in all he did. Whatever our gifts may be, God can find use for them even in the midst of our own prison. Whatever our situation, God can set us free.

For God's People in Bible Times

While Joseph was incarcerated, two new prisoners were added to his group: the cupbearer and the baker for the king of Egypt. Each had in some way displeased the king, and they were both dejected about their circumstances. But each man also had a dream about which he didn't know the meaning.

The cupbearer had dreamed he saw a vine with three branches. As soon as the vine budded, it blossomed and immediately turned into clusters of grapes. He squeezed them into the Pharaoh's cup, and there was instant wine.

Joseph explained to the men that God had given him a gift of interpreting dreams:

> *"The three branches are three days. Within three days Pharaoh will lift up your head and restore you to your position, and you will put Pharaoh's cup in his hand, just as you used to do when you were his cupbearer. But when all goes well with you, remember me and show me kindness; mention me to Pharaoh and get me out of this prison. For I was forcibly carried off from the land of the Hebrews, and even here I have done nothing to deserve being put in a dungeon."*
>
> —Genesis 40:12–15

Such a small request for such a positive prediction!

The baker, on the other hand, dreamed that he had three baskets of bread on top of his head. The baked goods were for Pharaoh, but birds were eating them quickly out of the basket. Joseph interpreted the baker's dream: *"The three baskets are three days. Within three days Pharaoh will lift off your head and hang you on a tree. And the birds will eat away your flesh"* (Genesis 40:18–19).

On the third day after the dreams, the Pharaoh celebrated his birthday by restoring the cupbearer and hanging the baker, just as Joseph had predicted. Now you might think the cupbearer would have been so elated at his release and at the accuracy of Joseph's interpretation that he would have immediately brought Joseph's name to Pharaoh's attention. But he didn't seem to give his time in jail another thought. He was free, and he forgot his promise to Joseph (verse 23).

For two years, Joseph languished in the prison with little hope of ever getting out. But the Lord was with him, and Joseph was at peace, despite his circumstances.

Consulting the Map

Joseph was in prison. While most of us doing this study will probably never be held in a prison like Joseph was kept in, many of us are in a prison of our own making. Our souls are (or have been) imprisoned in darkness — although this is not God's plan for us.

Scripture refers to the consequences of sin as darkness, but Jesus' perfect truth as light.

Read the following verses to discover what God says about the freedom He wants to give us.

Isaiah 42:6–7

_____

Isaiah 61:1

_____

2 Samuel 22:29

_____

2 Corinthians 4:6–9

_____

Ephesians 5:8

_____

Philippians 2:15

_____

Colossians 1:13

_____

1 Peter 2:9

_____

Jude 1:6

_____

Read John 8:32–36. Have you accepted the freedom Christ wants to give you, or are you still a slave to sin? In the space provided, briefly explain when you joined the family of God and were set free from the slavery of sin.

_____
_____
_____
_____
_____

One night the Pharaoh had two dreams that disturbed him. He sent for his magicians and wise men to help him unravel the meaning, but they had no answers for his confusion. Suddenly the cupbearer remembered Joseph: _"Today I am reminded of my shortcomings"_ (Genesis 41:9). He described the dreams that he and the baker had had in prison and the Hebrew slave who had interpreted them correctly: _"Things turned out exactly as he interpreted them to us: I was restored to my position, and the other man was hanged"_ (Genesis 41:13).

Pharaoh had Joseph brought to his court immediately. When he told Joseph that he understood that he could interpret dreams, Joseph replied humbly, _"I cannot do it...but God will give Pharaoh the answer he desires"_ (Genesis 41:16).

For Us in Today's World

It is difficult for me to imagine making such a selfless statement! If I had been in prison for years and had just been brought out because of some great gift I had, and then I was praised because of my abilities, I probably would be trying to promote myself as much as possible! But Joseph walked with God so closely that his natural response to Pharaoh's comment was to give God the glory. Don't you wish to be so close to God that you automatically react in a godly way? Joseph continued his intimate relationship with God while in prison — he walked with God in the darkness as well as in the light.

Are you in a dark place right now? Are you imprisoned by some situation in your life? Brother Lawrence, an uneducated, lowly member of the barefoot Carmelite order in Paris in the 1600s, was assigned to wash the pots and pans for the more learned brothers. Imagine the thought of never leaving the kitchen sink! Dishes day after day. How would *you* react?

Brother Lawrence is remembered because he walked so closely with God that he could pray, "Lord of all pots and pans and things, make me a saint by getting meals and washing up the plates."[1]

Brother Lawrence lived so abundantly in the presence of God that he could say:

> The time of business does not with me differ from the time of prayer, and in the noise and clatter of my kitchen, while several persons are at the same time calling for different things, I possess God in as great tranquility as if I were upon my knees at the blessed sacrament.[2]

In the letters that he wrote after his long days in the kitchen, Brother Lawrence taught others how to practice the presence of God despite adverse circumstances. He wrote:

> We cannot escape the dangers that abound in life without the actual and continual help of God. Let us, then, pray to Him for it continually. How can we pray to Him without being with Him? How can we be with Him but in thinking of Him often? And how can we often think of Him but by a holy habit which we should form of it? You will tell me that I am always saying the same thing. It is true, for this is the best and easiest method I know; and as I use no other, I advise all the world to do it. We must know before we can love. In order when we come to love Him, we shall also think of Him often, for our heart will be with our treasure. This is an argument which well deserves your consideration.[3]

This humble man, in our sight doomed to a life of washing pots, shows us that we can find God anywhere, and that we must discipline ourselves to practice His presence.

Joseph practiced the presence of God right where he was. He didn't say, "When I get out of here, I'll go to church," or "If You save me, God, I'll believe in You." Are our circumstances so much worse than Joseph's that we can't trust God to redeem us? Have we ever been thrown in a pit and left to die? Have we been pulled out, only to be sold by our brothers as a slave? Have we ever been thrown in jail and forgotten?

I once met a Southern beauty queen who had married a seminary student and was living "in the pits" — the pits being student housing. "My life is so miserable and my apartment so appalling that I refuse to unpack my wedding presents. This place isn't good enough for my dishes. We'll just eat on paper plates 'til I'm let out of this prison."

"How long will you be here?" I asked.

"For four long years."

"Are you planning to be miserable for four years?"

"There's no other choice. But when my husband gets his degree and we have our own church, then I'll be happy."

Will she really? If she practices misery for four years, will her husband's degree change her life? It has been shown that if you do anything consistently for thirty days, it will become a lifetime habit. What are you doing consistently?

Joseph and Brother Lawrence practiced the presence of God in the midst of the pits of life. They certainly wouldn't have waited to unpack the dishes!

Consulting the Map

Our culture today has made us think that we have to have everything instantly. We tap our foot when the microwave doesn't work as quickly as we think it should. We grumble over how long our computer takes to load a file, and we become almost hostile when our "fast food" is delivered a little more slowly than we expected. But despite what we might think is best, as we have seen in this study, and will continue to see, waiting is a part of God's plan. Read the following scriptures and do the basic math. Note how long each of the promises must have taken to be fulfilled.

MAN OF FAITH	SCRIPTURES	HOW MANY YEARS IT TOOK FOR THE COMPLETION OF THE PROMISE
Noah	Genesis 7:6; 8:13–14	_____
Abraham	Genesis 15:4–5; 16:15–16; 17:1; 17:17; 18:10; 21:5	_____
Moses	Exodus 3:17; 7:7; Deuteronomy 34:4–7	_____

As you can see, none of these plans of God's were completed quickly. If these great saints of the faith had to wait, why should we expect to be spared from this part of God's process? Clearly, His plan is different from the way we would do things.

Read Isaiah 55:8.

What does this verse say about how we do things and how God does them?

_____

_____

We have seen by example that God's plan often involves waiting. Now let's see what Scripture specifically says about it. Read the following verses and note what they say about waiting.

Psalm 37:34

_____

Psalm 69:3

_____

Proverbs 20:22

_____

Isaiah 8:17

_____

Having read these scriptures, the next time God is not moving as fast as you'd like, how do you hope to respond?

_____

_____

For God's People in Bible Times

Because Joseph was faithful in adverse circumstances, God rewarded him. Because he used his gifts to interpret Pharaoh's dream, he was set free. Because Joseph gave God the credit, Pharaoh put him in charge of the whole land of Egypt. Even though Pharaoh was not a believer, he could see that God was with Joseph, and he wanted to be on the winning side.

Perhaps you will recall that Joseph interpreted the Pharaoh's dream of seven fat cows and seven lean cows to mean that there would be seven years of plenty followed by seven years of famine. Joseph told Pharaoh that if Egypt stored up its surplus, it would be able to survive without starvation.

We know that God used the widespread famine to bring Joseph's brothers from Canaan to Egypt to buy grain — and to bring Joseph's childhood dream to fulfillment. There Joseph stood in robes of fine linen, with a gold chain around his neck and a signet ring on his finger, while his brothers bowed down before him, their faces to the ground. Joseph recognized them and was so moved at the sight of his long-lost brothers, evil though they had been, that he had to turn his head and weep.

Before he would let them go back home, Joseph told them he would keep Simeon until they returned with Benjamin, his only full brother. The scene that followed this request from the one they perceived to be the Egyptian ruler would be humorous if it were not so sadly typical of human nature.

For many years the brothers had deceived their father over the circumstances of Joseph's death. Because they had not been caught, they had eventually put their evil deeds behind them, but the guilt had been resting just below the surface. Isn't it amazing that even when we have sinned and gotten away with it, the guilt is still within us, keeping us from the full presence of God?

One brother said to the others, thinking Joseph couldn't understand their language, *"Surely we are being punished because of our brother. We saw how distressed he was when he pleaded with us for his life, but we would not listen; that's why this distress has come upon us"* (Genesis 42:21).

Suddenly they were thinking of Joseph, whom they hadn't seen in years. They felt God was punishing them for their sins. Then Reuben, wanting to make sure they remembered his one ounce of virtue, declared, *"Didn't I tell you not to sin against the boy? But you wouldn't listen! Now we must give an accounting for his blood"* (Genesis 42:22). In other words, if you had only listened to me, we wouldn't be in this mess!

How quickly we point the finger at others in time of trouble and remind them that this surely was not our fault! This sad, immature, guilt-ridden group had to go home and report their problems to their father, who was immediately distraught and depressed: *"Everything is against me!... You will bring my gray head down to the grave in sorrow"* (Genesis 42:36, 38). This mournful, melancholy message would have been enough even to instill guilt in an innocent group!

Consulting the Map

Reuben and his brothers knew they had done wrong, but to cover their actions they made excuses and rationalized. We tend to do the same thing when we make a poor choice or get caught in our sin.

Read the following verses, each containing an account of someone's making an excuse or rationalizing, and note God's reaction to the "blame game." Does it please Him or displease Him?

Exodus 3:9–12

_____

Exodus 4:10–14

_____

Exodus 32:21–35

_____

Jeremiah 1:6–7

_____

Luke 14:16–24

_____

_____

The next time you hear yourself placing the blame elsewhere, remember that God wants you to grow up and take responsibility for your own actions. Don't let excuses keep you from accepting God's call on your life.

> People are always blaming their circumstances for what they are. I don't believe in circumstances. The people who get on in this world are the people who look for the circumstances they want and if they cannot find them, make them.
>
> —George Bernard Shaw

As the months passed and the supply of grain dwindled, the brothers were forced to return to Egypt and take Benjamin with them, even though Jacob, their father, cried, *"Why did you bring this trouble on me by telling the man you had another brother?"* (Genesis 43:6).

When Joseph finally saw Benjamin, his own mother Rachel's son, he was so touched that he went to his room and wept. He never thought he would look upon his brother's face again. When Joseph finally got control of himself, he dismissed his servants from the room. When all except him and his brothers were gone, he cried out, *"I am your brother Joseph, the one you sold into Egypt!"* (Genesis 45:4). As they cowered, terrified before Joseph, he explained what had taken place since they had pulled him from the pit and sold him into slavery. Imagine their guilt as they relived the event from Joseph's point of view. Yet, just when they thought they would die of shame — or possibly at the hands of the Pharaoh — Joseph gave them unexpected relief. Instead of making them squirm in guilt, Joseph — the one who practiced the presence of God, even in prison — comforted them by saying, *"Do not be distressed and do not be angry with yourselves for selling me here, because it was to save lives that God sent me ahead of you"* (Genesis 45:5). What his brothers meant for evil, God meant for good. God was in control all along!

Joseph became the "savior" of his family, and he forgave their sins. How like Christ who, while we were yet sinners, died for us so that we might be saved. Joseph practiced the presence of God, both when in prison and when in power.

Joseph's family (all seventy of them) settled in the land of Goshen. His father, Jacob, lived there seventeen years until he died at the age of 147. His body was then taken back to Canaan to be buried in a cave in the field of Machpelah, where he was placed with Abraham, Sarah, Isaac, Rebekah, and his wife, Leah.

Jacob's story was ending, but the story of God's people had just begun. As the Jewish people still say, "May the God who blessed Abraham, Isaac, and Jacob bless you as well."

Trip Journal

1. Self-pity is often the basis for depression. How did Joseph handle the unfair treatment by his boss? In what areas do you feel self-pity today? Is life fair? Whom can you trust even when life seems unfair?

    When Joseph was in prison, he assessed his situation. What positive steps did he take? What can you do about your own circumstances?

2. What small request did Joseph make of the cupbearer after he interpreted his dream? How long was it before this man remembered his pledge to Joseph? How would you have responded in Joseph's place? How did Joseph behave?

3. What does it mean to "practice the presence of God"? How did Joseph do it? How did Brother Lawrence do it? How can you?

4. What have you practiced in life, good or bad, that has become a habit? What habits do you need to break? Can you discipline yourself for thirty days to stop this habit from controlling your life?

5. When you got away with something you knew you shouldn't have done, did you have a clear conscience? What happened to Joseph's brothers when they were put under pressure? Whom did they blame for their predicament? How did Reuben respond? Do you ever make those same human responses? In what circumstances?

6. If maturity includes the acceptance of blame and responsibility, where would you rank Joseph's brothers? Joseph? Yourself? Your mate? Your co-workers?

7. How did Jacob respond to the news that Benjamin had to go to Egypt? Why would Benjamin have been so special to him?

8. If you had been in Joseph's place and had these brothers bowing before you, what would you have wanted to do or say? What did Joseph do? How did he comfort their guilt?

Journey to Jesus:
A Glimpse of the Destination

Review the following chart on the comparison of Joseph as a "type" of Christ. Look up each scripture passage and write down any comparisons you see. Be sure to add any other ideas you or your group come up with in your study.

Joseph As a Type of Christ

JOSEPH		CHRIST
Genesis 37:3	Well-beloved son	Matthew 3:17
Genesis 37:13	Sent by his father	John 3:16
Genesis 37:5–9	Revealed his future position	Matthew 24:30–31
Genesis 37:19–20	Brothers plotted against him	Luke 20:13–14
Genesis 37:26–28	Sold for silver	Matthew 26:15
Genesis 39	Unyielding to temptation	Matthew 4:1–11
Genesis 39:13–18	Wrongfully accused	Matthew 26:59–65
Genesis 39:20	Put in the place of criminals	Luke 23:22–25
Genesis 41:14, 40	Raised up again	Ephesians 1:19–22
Genesis 41:42–44	Given power	Matthew 28:18
Genesis 47:25	Acknowledged as savior	Philippians 2:10–11
Genesis 45:1–15	Forgave wrongdoers	1 John 1:9

For Your Notebook

Add seven lean and seven fat cows to your list of sevens.

Referring to Genesis 11 through 50 and beginning with Terah, create a family tree in your notebook. Include all three of Terah's sons — Haran, Nahor, and Abraham — as well as their descendants.

Trip Snapshots
Looking Back — And Looking Forward

As we conclude our journey through Genesis, let's take a moment to review. First we saw God's power as He spoke the universe into being — heaven and earth; day and night; sky and water and land; seeds, plants, trees, and flowers; sun, moon, and stars; birds, fish, and animals; man and woman. We learned how God created Adam and Eve, the sacrament of marriage, and the institution of the family. We can see in Adam and Eve a foretelling of Christ, the Bridegroom, and His Bride, the Church.

In our walk, we also saw that after the Flood, the formation of different nations took place, and at the Tower of Babel, the beginning of different languages. Abraham was the founder of both the Hebrew and the Arab races through Isaac and Ishmael. Abraham, the father, was willing to sacrifice his beloved son, Isaac, just as centuries later, God the Father sacrificed His beloved Son, Jesus, so that we might have everlasting life.

Jacob, Isaac's son, struggled with God and came out a changed man, the founder of the twelve Hebrew tribes. Joseph, Jacob's favorite son, was rejected by his brothers and sold as a slave, and yet he continued to walk with God, forgiving those who wronged him just as Christ would later do with His enemies.

Besides the beginnings and foretellings, we have seen that God gives clear instructions to His children. He blesses those who obey and punishes those who don't. He both blessed and punished Adam and Eve, Abraham and Sarah, Isaac and Rebekah, Jacob and Rachel. He blessed Noah because he was a righteous man, and He took Enoch into heaven because he was a faithful man. He turned Lot's disobedient wife into a pillar of salt and blessed Joseph who walked closely with Him, even in difficult circumstances.

As the sins of the fathers are visited upon the children, so a thread of deception ran through these families. Adam and Eve hid the truth from God; Abraham lied by calling his wife his sister; Rebekah encouraged Jacob to deceive his father and brother; Jacob was deceived by his father-in-law, Laban, into marrying the wrong daughter; in turn, Laban was deceived by Jacob when he fled for home without telling his father-in-law. Jacob was deceived by his sons over the supposed death of Joseph, when, in fact, they had sold their brother into slavery. This family was hardly a trustworthy lot!

Through it all, however, they knew there was a God. They kept looking for Him in gardens, on walks, in the rain, at altars, in the wilderness and the desert, on mountains, at wells, in famines, on the rocks, in foreign lands, in struggles, in dreams, in prison, and in power.

How about you? As we have begun this journey to Jesus together, has God made a new beginning in your life? Have you obeyed Him and been blessed? Have you been deceptive or avoided the truth? Have you been slogging through the rain or struggling on the rocks? Are you and your family still looking for God in all the wrong places? Don't waste another moment in searching — ask the Lord to come into your life right now. Begin practicing the presence of God today — discipline yourself to walk closely with God.

LESSON 11

In Plagues and in the Passover

Read Exodus 1–15.

As we have traveled together from the Garden of Eden to the land of Egypt, we have observed that the book of Genesis is about beginnings and the book of Exodus is about a departure, a going out. Genesis shows us the Fall; Exodus, the redemption. Genesis is a family history; Exodus is the history of a nation. In Genesis, we saw that Jacob's family numbered seventy when they moved to Egypt but grew to over three million by the time Moses was ready to lead them out.

As we reflect on our own lives, we see that we have each had a beginning, each fallen into some kind of trouble, each tried to find a way out. Just as the Hebrews in Egyptian slavery were trying to escape, so we are seeking solutions for our problems. As they were looking for a savior, so we are all on a search for the God who will set us free.

How perfectly the Bible relates to you and me. How beautifully God tells the story of His people. How richly He fills the Old Testament with symbols, types, and predictions that culminate in the person of Jesus Christ, our Savior.

When I first committed my life to the Lord and began to study the Bible, I read the New Testament. I had always loved the stories of the Old Testament, but when I accepted Jesus, I wanted to spend my time with Him. But I began to realize in my study that I couldn't understand many of the references to Christ as the Lamb, the Light, the Bread, or the High Priest. Nor could I grasp the value of the sacrifice of His life or the power of His shed blood, without reading the Old Testament. I believed that Jesus had come to save me, but I had never connected His redemptive act with Noah's saving his family from the Flood, Abraham's saving Lot from Sodom and Gomorrah, Joseph's saving his family from starvation, and Moses' saving the Hebrews from slavery.

It was not until I began to read the Book of Beginnings that I saw how essential it was to know the history of the Hebrew people and their search for God. This background is necessary to have a real concept of why Jesus came to the earth as a man and shed His blood for you and me. I'd sung the hymn "There's Power in the Blood," but I had no idea what it meant or how I could ever be "cleansed by the blood of the Lamb." Neither thought was either appealing or significant to me, but as I looked into the Old Testament, both Genesis and Exodus showed me God's pattern, and the pieces began to fit together. The puzzle I'd been struggling with suddenly made sense, and I began to see the whole picture.

Let's move ahead 400 years, as I share with you my enthusiasm for God's miraculous plans for our lives and my excitement over finding Him.

For God's People in Bible Times

In God's covenant with Abraham, He had predicted that His people would be slaves in a foreign land for 400 years (see Genesis 15:13). That prophecy came true after Joseph's life had ended. Because God blessed His people:

> *Their descendants were very fertile, increasing rapidly in numbers; there was a*
> *veritable population explosion so that they soon became a large nation, and they*
> *filled the land of Goshen. Then, eventually, a new king came to the throne of*
> *Egypt who felt no obligation to the descendants of Joseph.*
> —Exodus 1:7–8, TLB

Because he feared their numbers and their prosperity, Pharaoh made slaves of the Hebrews and put cruel taskmasters over them. But amazingly, the worse they were treated, the more they multiplied. Pharaoh instructed the Hebrew midwives to kill all the newborn boys in order to curb the population, but because these women believed in God, they wouldn't perform such a heinous act. A beautiful boy was born to a family in the tribe of Levi, and his parents hid him at home for three months to keep him safe. Finally, his mother made a little basket, waterproofed it with tar, laid the baby in it, and placed it in the weeds along the water's edge. This is where he was soon found by a princess, one of Pharaoh's daughters. She was immediately captivated by the baby and took him as her own, naming him *Moses* — which means "to draw out" — because she had taken him out of the water. In an ironic twist of fate that demonstrates that God was truly in control, she hired his very own mother to be his nurse. For forty years, Moses lived like a king, even receiving his education in the courts of Pharaoh. But one day, when he saw an Egyptian mistreating a Hebrew slave, he reacted with violence, killing the Egyptian, and then in fear for his own life, Moses fled the country.

Moses came to a well in Midian and took a rest to mull over his future. When seven daughters of the local priest came by, he helped them water their flocks and they invited him home for dinner. Moses eventually decided to settle in Midian. He married a woman named Zipporah, and they had a baby named *Gershom,* whose name means "foreigner." Midian had been named for one of Abraham's sons by his later wife, Keturah; Midian is located on the eastern arm of the Red Sea in what is today's Jordan.

In the meantime, the plight of the Hebrews in Egypt became worse, and eventually the time came for God to fulfill His promise to Abraham: *"I will punish the nation that enslaves them, and at the end they will come away with great wealth"* (Genesis 15:14, TLB).

When Moses had been in Midian forty years, God appeared to him in a burning bush. He told Moses to take his shoes off because he was standing on holy ground: *"I am the God of your fathers — the God of Abraham, Isaac, and Jacob"* (Exodus 3:6, TLB). Moses had never before met God personally, although his Hebrew childhood training had taught him to believe in the traditional God. Moses hid his face in awe and terror.

Oswald Chambers wrote:

> If we have never had the experience of taking our commonplace religious shoes off our commonplace religious feet, and getting rid of all the undue familiarity with which we approach God, it is questionable whether we have ever stood in His presence.[1]

We may be religious and even refer to the Lord as our "Friend," but if we have never dropped to our knees because of the overwhelming power of His majesty, if we have never taken our shoes off because we know we're on His holy ground, perhaps we have never found the real God, the King of kings. Moses wasn't even looking for God, but he was awestruck when God spoke to him: "I've chosen you to go back into Egypt and set My people free."

There is no one more shocked than a "nominal" believer who's been living a good life, when he suddenly hears God speak clearly and give him an assignment. *God, I didn't mean to believe in You that much! Surely You don't mean me.*

But God did mean Moses. He had been preparing Moses for eighty years to be the leader of His people. Moses had grown up in the palace and had learned the structure of Egyptian government, but he had also been trained by his own biological mother in the ways of the God of the Hebrews. Despite his preparation, Moses was not eager to rise to his calling. But God countered every excuse Moses gave. When Moses complained that he wasn't a good speaker, God agreed to send his brother, Aaron, as a mouthpiece. Moses responded by wondering what the people would think when he would say, "I AM has sent me."

To overcome Moses' fear of rejection, God demonstrated His miraculous power by turning Moses' staff into a snake and making his hand white with leprosy, and then returning them both to normal. When Moses saw the power of God demonstrated right before his eyes, he made the commitment to go back to Egypt and lead the people to freedom.

When Moses and Aaron arrived in Egypt, they went first to the Hebrew elders and performed miracles to establish their credentials as messengers from God. The people, who were worn down from overwork, and whose spirits were depressed from servitude and slavery, rejoiced that God had indeed sent help. There was a way out, an exodus, although it wasn't an easy route. As God had said about Pharaoh, *"I will make him stubborn so that he will not let the people go"* (Exodus 4:21, TLB).

When Moses demanded that Pharaoh "let my people go," Pharaoh's first response was to insist on the same production quota for the bricks that the Hebrews were making, but to give them no straw. When the Hebrews couldn't produce the required bricks, the taskmasters beat them.

Suddenly Moses didn't look like a man from God anymore. Moses tried to review the plan for them, but they wouldn't listen. He lost heart himself and cried out to God, *"Why did you ever send me, if you were going to do this to them?"* (Exodus 5:22, TLB). *"My own people won't even listen to me any more; how can I expect Pharaoh to? I'm no orator!"* (Exodus 6:12, TLB).

Consulting the Map

Moses often reviewed his weaknesses to himself and to God. He was disappointed with the gift that God had given him. If a child receives a gift that they do not like, they may throw it across the room and pout because it was not the gift they wanted. Parents of such a child are ashamed when the child acts this way — especially if they do so in the presence of the giver. As adults, we may have learned better "manners" and do not insult the giver to their face. Yet, when we minimize the gifts God has given us, that is exactly what we are doing!

God called Moses to a mission, yet Moses did not see what he had been given as a gift, and so he had a little temper tantrum. He was discontented with God's plan for his life. God does not always give us the bigger picture.

Read the following scriptures and in your own words, write how each person seemed to feel about God's plan for their life.

Jonah 4

_____

_____

1 Kings 19:13–14

_____

_____

Read Isaiah 55:8.
What does this verse say about our plans versus God's plans?

_____

_____

While God's ways and ours may be different, God does see the big picture. Read Revelation 15:3 and note what it says about God's ways.

_____

_____

Have you found this to be true in your own life? Sometimes you feel God telling you to do something, yet you feel that you cannot do it and you are discontent with God's plan for your life. Yet, later you see the bigger picture, and you know that God was right all along. Briefly explain the situation as it may have occurred in your own life.

_____

_____

_____

_____

_____

How will this awareness alter your reaction the next time you feel God prompting you to do something?

_____

_____

How often do we get excited over some plan God has for us, and then when it doesn't seem to work out easily and we face more adversity than we expected, we cry out, "Why did You do this to me? Why didn't You send someone else?" When have you experienced this in your own life?

_____

_____

_____

God grieves over this kind of "wailing" from His people, and so He told Moses how to approach Pharaoh and what Aaron should say. God forewarned Moses, telling him that the process would not be easy. God wanted the Exodus to demonstrate His almighty power and be an event that would never be forgotten.

Moses was eighty years old when he began the fight against Pharaoh. God caused Moses to be able to perform miracles that, at first glance, the court magicians were able to duplicate, but there was an important difference. When Aaron's rod became a serpent, so did the magicians', but Aaron's serpent ate up theirs. Unfortunately, Pharaoh was not impressed then or later when Moses turned the rivers into blood or when the palace was filled with frogs. But when the dust turned into lice, infesting the people and the animals, and when swarms of flies infiltrated each room in every home, Pharaoh began to weaken, and he told Moses that the Hebrews could go worship their God if God would stop the plagues. But each time God called off the plagues, Pharaoh would not keep his promise to let the Hebrews go.

God caused the flocks of the Egyptians to die while keeping the animals of the Hebrews immune from the plague. Although Pharaoh could clearly see what was happening, he wouldn't give in — not even when boils broke out on every single Egyptian. Neither a hailstorm — the worst in history — nor a swarm of locusts that covered the face of the earth and blotted out the sun could convince the Pharaoh. Three days of darkness — while the Hebrews lived and worked in the light — caused the Egyptians to cry out to their Pharaoh for relief, and he offered to let Moses and his people leave without their flocks and herds. "All or nothing at all" was Moses' reply as he prepared his people for flight. God instructed them to ask their Egyptian neighbors for gold and silver jewelry and to get ready for their exodus, thus fulfilling the prophecy that they would leave with much wealth after their four hundred years in slavery.

As a child, I had memorized the order of the ten plagues, and as an adult, I knew of the Passover as a Jewish holiday, but I had never seen these events as significant to me or as a part of any great plan of God for His people. Once I began to study the Old Testament with spiritual eyes, I was in awe of the miracles God had done despite the human reactions of His cast of characters.

When Moses announced that God was about to kill the firstborn in every Egyptian home, even the firstborn of each animal, unless Pharaoh let the people go, the stubborn ruler still refused his request, and the Hebrews wondered how God would know their homes from those of the Egyptians.

Once again, it was up to Moses to explain God's plan of provision to the people — God's way of salvation for those who would believe. In Exodus 12, we read of God's detailed instructions to Moses. As was true in the case of Noah, God the Father gave very specific steps to follow. He never says, "Go do your own thing;" instead He says, "Do it My way and be blessed." Noah built the ark to code and became the savior of his family and the entire human race. Now it was Moses' turn to be the savior of his people and bring them from slavery into freedom.

Even though God had been the moving force in sending the plagues and sparing the Hebrews, these descendants of Abraham, Isaac, and Jacob were still looking for God in all the wrong places. They couldn't see God's hand in the flies or the frogs, the locusts or the lice. But when God was ready to perform a miracle — a miracle so great it is still celebrated today — they heard His voice. They found God in the Passover and followed His clear instructions as Moses explained them.

Each Hebrew father was to provide a year-old lamb, a perfect lamb without spot or blemish, for his family. He was to kill this lamb and place the blood of the lamb on the upper doorframe of the house. He was to take a cluster of hyssop (a common weed), dip it in the blood, and strike it against the lintel above the door and on each side. Just draining the blood into the basin wasn't enough; it had to be applied, placed where it could be seen. God said, *"When I see the blood I will pass over you and I will not destroy your firstborn children when I smite the land of Egypt"* (Exodus 12:13, TLB).

Each father was to present the roasted lamb to his family for their evening meal, being careful not to break the bones of the animal. If any of the lamb was left, it had to be burned. Nothing was to be saved for the next day. The father was to provide the lamb and apply the blood, and the entire family was to eat for nourishment and strength.

The bread for the meal was to be prepared with no leaven (yeast being a symbol for sin), that the family might be ready to leave at a moment's notice. They also were to eat bitter herbs as a sign of suffering.

Consulting the Map

The Hebrew families were instructed to eat a good meal to prepare themselves for their trip. Likewise, as we head off to continue on our journey to Jesus, we need nourishment; we need to feed on God's Word.

Review the following scriptures and note what each verse refers to as our food.

Deuteronomy 8:3

_____

Psalm 119:103

_____

Jeremiah 15:16

_____

Ezekiel 2:8

_____

Ezekiel 3:1–3

_____

Matthew 4:4

_____

John 6:51–58

_____

1 Corinthians 10:3–4

_____

1 Peter 2:2

_____

Congratulations! Participating in this study by reading and studying God's Word is a very effective way to nourish yourself spiritually. Based on what you have learned from the verses above, list other ways in which you receive spiritual nourishment.

_____

_____

_____

_____

Now go back over your list and place a number one (1) next to the method that is the most effective form of nourishment for you, a two (2) next to the second, and so on.

Just like some people do better with carbohydrates and others are better with protein, so it is with our spiritual food. Once you focus on which form of nourishment works the best for you, you can work to be sure that you take in some of that daily.

Before partaking of the meal, each family member was to be dressed in traveling clothes with their bags packed, ready for the journey. They were to eat hurriedly while standing, prepared to go into the wilderness.

The people believed Moses and were amazingly cooperative. And at midnight, there went up a cry from each Egyptian home as God caused each firstborn son to die. By morning, grief pervaded the land. This time Pharaoh insisted that the Hebrews leave _immediately,_ and the Egyptians gave them gold jewelry, clothing, and riches as farewell presents. The sons of Jacob had been in the land of Egypt for 430 years when Pharaoh finally said, "I'll let the people go." God wanted His people to remember this event each year, so He set aside a time of celebration: The Feast of the Passover. All Hebrews were to commemorate this miracle with a seven-day celebration. No yeast was to be used or even allowed in the home during these seven days. This permanent law is still obeyed today in orthodox Jewish homes throughout Passover, as they remember how God passed over their homes and saved them from destruction.

As the Hebrew people looked up to God that night and did as He instructed in order to be saved, so can we look to Him for salvation today. God gave Moses a roadmap that led to the salvation of His people, and we have such a roadmap today.

For Us in Today's World

God provided His Son, Jesus, as our perfect sacrificial Lamb. You are redeemed *with the precious blood of Christ, as of a lamb without blemish and without spot* (1 Peter 1:19, KJV). *For Christ, our Passover lamb, has been sacrificed* (1 Corinthians 5:7).

As God has made provision for our salvation through the shed blood of His Son, we must take hold of this offering and apply the blood to our lives. The blood alone didn't save the Hebrews, for it wasn't until they placed it on their homes that the angel of death would pass them by. Head knowledge alone of God's plan wasn't enough; they had to act on it, apply it, make it a part of their lives. So it is with us — just knowing there is a God is not enough to save us. We must accept Jesus as our personal Lord and Savior, and apply His blood to our sin-stained hearts.

As God provides the sacrifice and we apply His Son's blood, we are then to take in His Word as food for our souls. Jesus said, *"Just as the living Father sent me and I live because of the Father, so the one who feeds on me will live because of me"* (John 6:57). We must feed on God's Word so that we will never hunger.

If we are to continue on in our fellowship with God, we must also search our lives and root out any hidden sin: *"Be on your guard against the yeast of the Pharisees and Sadducees"* (Matthew 16:6). Paul explained to the Corinthians, who were believing Christians but who had not yet purged out their old habits and nature, that they had to take action:

> *Don't you know that a little yeast works through the whole batch of dough? Get rid of the old yeast that you may be a new batch without yeast — as you really*

are. For Christ, our Passover lamb, has been sacrificed. Therefore let us keep the Festival, not with the old yeast, the yeast of malice and wickedness, but with bread without yeast, the bread of sincerity and truth.

—1 Corinthians 5:6–8

As we purge that old leaven — the yeast of sin — from our lives, we can remember the bitter herbs the Hebrews ate that night, and realize that the Christian life is not without heartache and suffering: *Endure hardship as discipline; God is treating you as sons* (Hebrews 12:7). *God disciplines us for our good, that we may share in his holiness: No discipline seems pleasant at the time, but painful. Later on, however, it produces a harvest of righteousness and peace for those who have been trained by it* (Hebrews 12:10–11).

Christ suffered for us and drank the bitter cup of death that we might have everlasting life; yet He, like the Passover lamb, had none of his bones broken: *These things happened so that the scripture would be fulfilled: "Not one of his bones will be broken"* (John 19:36; see also Psalm 34:20).

In order to respond to God when He calls, we must be ready to move. We are not to sit idly by, waiting for some bolt of lightning to jolt us into action, but we are to be prepared. The Hebrews had to trust that God would spare them, but they took him at His word and got ready. They stood up while they ate, they had on their walking shoes, they were ready to go. Are you ready to go? When God calls on you, will you say, "Here am I, send me"? Oswald Chambers wrote:

> When God speaks, many of us are like men in a fog, we give no answer.... Be ready for the sudden surprise visits of God. A ready person never needs to get ready. Think of the time we waste trying to get ready when God has called.[2]

Consulting the Map

Just as the people had to be ready to leave Egypt, so we are instructed to be ready. But for what? I am always ready to go to lunch or to go shopping, but that is not what God is asking!

Read the following verses to see what God says about our preparedness.

Luke 21:36

_____

Ephesians 6:18

_____

2 Timothy 4:2

_____

Titus 1:8

_____

1 Peter 3:15

_____

The final passage listed, 1 Peter 3:15, addressed our telling people about the hope we have in Christ. In the space below, write out the answer you would give to someone who asks you about your Christian hope.

_____

_____

_____

_____

The Hebrews had been looking for God to save them from slavery and set them free, and He did. He passed over each home marked with the blood of the lamb and told them never to forget what He had done:

> _"Again I say, this celebration shall identify you as God's people, just as much as if his brand of ownership were placed upon your foreheads. It is a reminder that the Lord brought us out of Egypt with great power."_
>
> —Exodus 13:16, TLB

As God's mark was on the Hebrews in the past, it will be on all believers in the future. The book of Revelation states that harm was to come only to those _who did not have the mark of God's seal on their foreheads_ (Revelation 9:4, TEV).

As we believe in God's power today and accept His salvation, we are marked in God's sight:

When you heard the true message, the Good News that brought you salvation...you believed in Christ, and God put his stamp of ownership on you by giving you the Holy Spirit he had promised.

—Ephesians 1:13, TEV

The Spirit is God's mark of ownership on you (Ephesians 4:30, TEV). We can't see this mark on each other, but God can. His all-seeing eyes look down on us, and He knows those who are His. The Shepherd knows His sheep.

Consulting the Map

Like a shepherd knows his sheep, God knows us, and we are His. If He is our Shepherd, we must follow Him as His sheep. Addressing this topic, Charles Spurgeon had this to say: "We should follow our Lord as unhesitatingly as sheep follow their shepherd, for *He has a right to lead us wherever He pleases.* We are not our own, we are bought with a price — let us recognize the rights of the redeeming blood."[3]

Read the following verses and note what God's Word says about following Christ, our Shepherd.

John 10:14

_____

John 10:27

_____

John 12:26

_____

As His sheep, we must follow Him. But what does that mean to us today? Do you remember when, as a child, you played follow the leader? What did you do? You imitated the leader's movements as closely as you could. Likewise, when we follow Christ, we do what He does.

Read Philippians 2:5 and note what it says about being like Christ.

_____

Read the following verses and note what actions of Christ's we should imitate.

Matthew 20:28

_____

Luke 4:43

_____

Luke 19:10

_____

Which of the above actions do you feel God is calling you to imitate? Write a brief prayer below asking God to help you be more like Christ in this way.

_____

_____

_____

When you enter Disneyland, your hand is stamped. You usually can't see the mark, but if you wish to leave and then return, the guard places your hand under a special light and "the stamp of ownership" appears before your very eyes. So it is with God's kingdom. He has placed His mark on us, and His special light shines down and shows up on his saints.

As a further encouragement to the people He had saved, God led them by a cloud by day and a pillar of fire by night, giving tangible evidence of His abiding presence. Don't we often think today, _If only I could see God or some sign of His reality, then I could believe?_ The Hebrews could see proof right in front of them, and although at first it excited them, as they plodded through the wilderness carrying everything they could manage — along with the bones of Joseph — they became weary and began to complain to Moses: "Have you brought us out here to die in the desert because there were not enough graves for us in Egypt? Why did you make us leave Egypt?"

Isn't it amazing how quickly they lost sight of God, took their minds off of His miracles, and began to cry, "Poor little me! Oh, for the good ol' days in Egypt!"?

As Pharaoh and his armies pursued them, the Hebrews headed straight for the Red Sea. If dying in the desert looked bad, drowning in the depths of the sea looked even worse. Moses called out to the Lord for a new roadmap for their salvation, but God answered, "Quit praying and get the people moving! Forward march!" Has God ever had to say that to you as you sat weeping and wailing over the deep waters in front of you? "Quit praying and get moving! It's easier for Me to push you if you're already in motion!"

The people had little faith that God in His cloud could save them, but because they had no alternative plan, they headed for the sea. That night, God placed His pillar of fire between the pursuing Egyptians and the Hebrews, blinding the Egyptians and giving warm light to His people all at the same time. In the morning, Moses stretched his rod over the sea, and the Lord opened up a dry path with high walls of water on each side.

Do you look for God when you're in deep waters? Are you often out to sea or — as my mother used to say — stuck in a boat without a paddle? God does the most amazing things when we believe in Him in seemingly unbelievable situations. Not only did He save His people, but He also drowned their enemies! Now that's a God who has placed the mark of ownership on His people — a God who separates the saints from the sinners.

Consulting the Map

The people Moses was leading did not have a strong faith. They were weak, but God worked anyway.

We are weak, but Christ is strong. Is this a problem we need to overcome? As humans, we tend to think of weakness as a fault. Read the following verses to see how God views our weakness.

1 Corinthians 4:10

_____

_____

2 Corinthians 12:9

_____

_____

The Message version of 2 Corinthians 13:9 puts it this way: *We couldn't possibly do otherwise. We don't just put up with our limitations; we celebrate them, and then go on to celebrate every strength, every triumph of the truth in you. We pray hard that it will all come together in your lives.* Instead of being afraid of your weakness, celebrate it and allow Christ to be your strength.

Many of us wander around in the desert waiting for God to lift us up to a mountaintop experience. Surely the murmuring and disputing Hebrews, still longing for the good ol' days of Egypt, were ready for some excitement. They had wandered through the Sinai Peninsula for three months when God called Moses to the mountaintop and offered him a new contract. As always, God wanted to give clear instructions and have the people obey. If they would follow His commandments, He would make the Hebrews a kingdom of priests, a holy nation — a special people.

Moses went down from the mountain to prepare the people to meet God face to face. They even washed all their clothes so that they would be clean before a righteous God. On the morning of the third day, a huge thunderstorm rolled in, a big black cloud settled on the mountain, a ram's horn blasted, the whole mountain shook, and God spoke in a deep voice, calling Moses to the mountaintop.

Surely the people would be positive, accepting, faithful believers after meeting God on the mountaintop.

Trip Journal

1.   Do you remember ever being so in awe of God's presence in your life that you took off your spiritual shoes and said, "This is holy ground"? Do you agree with Oswald Chambers that if you haven't felt this way, "it is questionable whether [you] have ever stood in His presence"? How does this feeling of awe compare with other people talking of having a "spiritual experience"?

2.   What plans has God ever revealed to you personally? What steps have you taken toward those plans? How easy or difficult were those steps? Have you ever cried out, "This is too hard, Lord. Send someone else!"? Can you see that if the way is easy, God gets no credit?

3. To what have you or some member of your family ever been a slave? Have there been addictions or compulsions? Did you find a person like Moses to set you free? A prescription or a human plan to release you? A spiritual victory beyond human ability? What healings have you experienced?

4. Are there any people you know who are never content? What have you tried to do for them that has failed? What occasionally robs you of your own joy? How do you apply the strength of Christ to your moment of discouragement?

5. Are you ready to leave your Egypt? Your place of bondage? Your past life? Your emotional pain?

For Your Notebook

Write down the five steps of the Passover and then answer the following questions for yourself.

PROVIDE: Have you accepted Jesus as your sacrificial Lamb, which God has provided for your salvation?

PLACE: Have you incorporated God's plan into your life? Have you applied it to your situation and circumstances?

PRESENT: Do you present God's Word to yourself and others?

PURGE: Are you willing to let God purge you of past problems and bad habits?

PREPARE: Are you preparing yourself to know God in a more intimate way this year than ever before?

Add the seven daughters of Midian to your list of sevens.

Start a list of forties, the number of probation and testing.
• It rained forty days and forty nights (Genesis 7:12).
• Isaac was forty years old when he married Rebekah (Genesis 25:20).
• Esau was forty years old when he married his Hittite wives (Genesis 26:34).
• Moses was on the mountain forty days and nights (Exodus 24:18).
• The Israelites ate manna for forty years (Exodus 16:35).

Trip Snapshots
Looking Back — And Looking Forward

Before we move on, let's check our map. We want to make sure we have followed our scheduled route and not made a wrong turn along the way. Let's pause by an oasis in the desert and reflect on our personal progress.

During our journey from the Garden of Eden through the Red Sea, we have seen several principles that have been repeated often enough to catch our attention.

• God doesn't ask a lot of us. He's not unreasonable, and He expects obedience and honesty.
• When God's people follow His clear directions, He blesses them, provides for them, and saves them.
• When God's people are deceptive or otherwise disobey Him, He punishes them, forgives them, and teaches them.

What simple truths! What wonderful principles to use in the raising of our own children.

We have visited some of the right places where people in the Bible and in today's world look for God. We've become acquainted with some of the heroes of faith, great men and women with human personalities, strengths, and weaknesses, called by God to lead and save their people.

1. We started in the lush Garden of Eden where Adam and Eve walked and talked with God. We saw that Eve had everything she could possibly want, yet she reached out for something more. She knew God's one rule clearly, and yet she disobeyed. She was easily beguiled. She knew she was in the wrong, yet she tried to deceive God. Her husband knew right from wrong, but he went along with her idea.

How about you? Are you content with what you have until God provides more? Do you know when you are being tempted or beguiled? Do you know at least one area of your life in which God is disciplining you into obedience? Are you willing to put aside any deceptive ploys and stop compromising your standards to go along with the crowd?

If your answers are all positive, you may move ahead. But you can't leave the Garden until you've learned to be obedient to His simple directions for your life.

2. As you stroll out into the fields, you will remember meeting Cain, a strong-willed and rebellious man who wasn't about to obey God. He had not learned the lesson of his parents in the Garden. He wasn't interested in fostering family relationships, and he surely didn't want to be responsible for his brother. Think for a moment about your own life. There may have been a few times in the past when you wanted your own way. Perhaps you are always the one who has to give in and take care of other people. In frustration, have you ever said, as Cain did, "Am I my brother's keeper?"

When you read these sentences, do you see some need for improvement in your attitude toward others? Are you willing to look for opportunities to be of assistance to your brothers in need? Are you willing to be pleasant to someone you don't even like? Knowing the principle of reaping and sowing, are you ready to evaluate what you are planting in the fields? *The one who sows to please his sinful nature, from that nature will reap destruction; the one who sows to please the Spirit, from the Spirit will reap eternal life* (Galatians 6:8).

As you review these questions, decide if you are ready to move on to the next stop on your journey to Jesus, or if you need to stay out in the field to improve the quality of your seeds before planting again.

3. If you've learned to obey God and care for your brothers, you are ready for a long walk with Enoch. Not much was written about Enoch, perhaps because he was a godly man who caused no trouble. Decent people don't make good press, but Enoch impressed God so much that God didn't wait for him to die; He translated him into heaven to be with Him.

How about you? Are you inhaling and exhaling the very breath of God? Are you in stride with God? Do you exercise with Him each day? Do you need to spend more time in God's Word to get to know Him better?

There's no point in looking for God if you have no time to walk with Him when you find Him. If you're not satisfied with your Christian walk, pause and pray until God gives you some insight on the closeness of your walk with Him.

4. Now that you are breathing in harmony with God, you are ready to review the lessons learned from Noah, another godly man, who was obedient to the Father's instructions down to the last gangplank and pigeon. He built an ark when there was no rain, and he had faith that God knew what He was doing, even when there was no evidence. He was patient throughout the time he spent in the ark, and the minute he got free, he built an altar to worship God. Noah was surely a righteous man, one we should think about each time we see a rainbow of promise.

As you consider the lessons from Noah's life, how do you think his dedication and obedience compare with your own?

What's the longest you've been cooped up in one place? How did you react? Do you need to develop your patience?

When you finish an arduous task, do you stop to worship God? Are your prayers full of thanksgiving?

How does your faith compare to that of Noah, a man who was willing to be ridiculed in order to obey God's instructions?

What kind of an ark is God asking you to build? Are you ready to follow His instructions to the letter? Don't move until you're sure, or you might drown in the Flood.

5. Now that your faith has been strengthened and the waters have receded, you can move ahead to the Tower of Babel. God the Father had brought up His children well, provided them with gardens and rainbows, and still they didn't give Him any respect, credit, or praise. He had created their talents and endowed them with ministry gifts, and yet they got so caught up in their own success that they went out to build a monument — not to God, but to themselves.

How often do you give God credit for the intelligence and abilities He has bestowed upon you? Have you ever followed a person instead of God? What personal lesson does God have for you in the Tower of Babel? What confusion in your life right now needs to be healed before you move on? What monuments have you been building to yourself?

6. Now that you've taken down those mental statues of yourself, you are able to focus your attention on God.

When Abraham heard God's call, he packed up everything and started to move, even though he didn't know where God was guiding him. It's always easier for God to give us momentum when we're already moving. Because Abraham trusted God and had faith in His directions, God made him the father of many nations. Abraham was so obedient to God's directions that he was willing to offer his son on the altar as a sacrifice to God.

How in tune are you to God's voice? What was the last instruction that you knew came from God? How did you react? Do you need to take some time to practice your faith and build your trust in God? Aren't you glad God forgives? Tell Him right now why you need forgiveness. Confess any of your actions that are displeasing to God.

Before you can move forward in your search for God, you must bolster your faith and recheck your obedience and honesty. Are you in the wilderness right now? Do you not know which way to turn? Is the lure of Egypt calling to you?

Remember Abraham: He didn't move until he heard God's voice. But the minute Abraham got the call, he headed off, trusting God to direct his path. God asks us to believe in Him and not lean on our own understanding. Are you ready to pack up and move when God gives the call?

7. How would you like to be named "the Deceiver" — and then live up to your title?! Jacob just seemed to attract trouble. His mother, Rebekah, manipulated his life and kept him around the house. We can be grateful that he was ever able to grow up and get married at all!

Do you still have a parent who has emotional control over you? Do you have parents or in-laws who use you as a pawn in their games? Have you sometimes been deceptive and worked one parent against the other?

In Genesis, God tells us that when we marry, we are to "leave and cleave," both emotionally and physically. He doesn't want adult children still tied to their parents. If you have a parent problem, pause and ask the Lord for direction. As an adult, Jacob still did what his mother told him to do, even though it violated a clear ruling of God; he just went along to avoid confrontation. How often we see someone compromise what they know to be God's standards in order to avoid a potential problem. Don't be a victim of the easy way out. Listen to God's plan for your life.

Jacob was forced to leave home because of his deception. But God knew he was a good man, so He met Jacob on the rocks face to face in an awesome place. If you're on the rocks today, look up. This could be a new beginning for you. This could be your "gate to heaven." Move on!

8. For Jacob, it was love at first sight when he met Rachel, and he was willing to do anything to get her for his wife, including working fourteen years for no money! During the time Jacob lived on his father-in-law's land, he and Laban deceived each other. There must be a reason that we become so easily deceptive — and so easily deceived. Think back to the last time you told a "white lie." Why did you do it? How do you feel about it now?

What could the Church do to increase awareness of the need for honesty and integrity? Is there someone right now to whom you need to go and straighten out some past problems? Remember God's words: *No one who practices deceit will dwell in my house; no one who speaks falsely will stand in my presence* (Psalm 101:7).

Does someone have a grudge against you, something that you need to repair?

It is so easy for Christians to look good in church while harboring ill will toward one another. It is so natural to see our side of a situation and not be willing to take the first step toward healing.

Jesus Himself said:

> *"I tell you that anyone who is angry with his brother will be subject to judgment.... Therefore, if you are offering your gift at the altar and there remember that your brother has something against you, leave your gift there in front of the altar. First go and be reconciled to your brother; then come and offer your gift."*
>
> —Matthew 5:22–24

Today could be a turning point in your human relationships. Be the one to take the first step.

9. With all the problems that Joseph had as a teenager, it's a miracle that he grew up to be such a balanced and godly man. Before you walk on toward God, check your past. Were you

rejected, molested, unloved, or deprived as a child? Do you have some emotional weights of the past that you need to shed? Seek out a trusted friend or counselor and begin to deal with these past pains.

Chances are, you haven't been in jail, yet you may be a prisoner in some other set of circumstances. You may be locked in an alcoholic home, you may be suffering in a difficult marriage, you may be serving time for some emotional pains of the past. Many of us are in the chains and fetters of financial burdens that keep us from enjoying the freedom the Lord promises: *Then you will know the truth, and the truth will set you free* (John 8:32).

When Joseph went to prison for a crime he did not commit, what did he do? He didn't run and hide. He didn't deny he was there and sink into a false world of unreality. And he didn't wallow in self-pity. Instead, he faced the facts, undeserved as they were, and refused to waste energy on hatred and bitterness. He thanked God that he was alive and developed a plan of how to make the best of an unexpected tragedy. Here was an innocent man persecuted for his exemplary behavior.

Does his situation sound at all like yours? Not all punishment is deserved, and those of us who are victimized in any way have to make a decision whether to sit and cry, hating those who have done us wrong, or formulate the best possible plan, praise God, and move on. We can focus either on the prison bars on the windows or on the sky beyond.

Are you in a prison today? Is some guard trying to whip you into shape? Take a realistic view of your options, decide if you need some counsel, and move a few steps toward the door. Practice the presence of God, whether in prison or in power. The truth will set you free.

10. Moses had been trained in the Pharaoh's palace for a position of leadership, but as you will remember, he'd gotten himself in trouble and left town to escape the consequences. Starting a new life, he soon settled into the safety of the status quo, where he was leading nothing more complex than a flock of sheep. Moses knew about God, but he hadn't been actively seeking to know God in a personal way. His basic needs in life were being met, and he had no urgency to seek spiritual direction.

Does any of this have a familiar ring? Are you a "good person" who's content to stay out of trouble and toe the middle line? Do you have some talent that you're not currently using?

Does God see you as a potential leader? Perhaps He is calling you as He did Moses. Will you reply, "Who me? You must have the wrong person!" Will you be as surprised as Moses was when God taps your shoulder and sends you to go and save His people?

Each one of us can be a leader in the area of our own experience. Those of us who have suffered and have triumphed over tragedy can use our trials to give hope to others. Remember, the God of peace comforts us, not so we'll become comfortable, but so we will comfort others.

What potential for leadership do you have? Are you available for training so that you'll be ready when God calls? Don't just sit around with the sheep. Stand up and say, "Here am I. Send me."

In reviewing these ten stories based on the lives of Old Testament men and women, we've had a chance to examine our own personality, our own attitudes, our own character, our own patience, our own honesty, our own obedience, and our own willingness to heed God's call. Now that we've looked at who we are and have felt the touch of God, we're ready to take those steps necessary to stand in the very presence of God. Let's continue on our journey to Jesus.

> *If the LORD delights in a man's way,*
> *he makes his steps firm;*
> *though he stumble, he will not fall,*
> *for the LORD upholds him with his hand.*

—Psalm 37:23–24

Scenic Overlook

When I spoke at an international business conference in Amsterdam, I met an Englishman named Reginald. He identified himself as a Christian and told me how he had found God. During World War II, his battalion was trained to cross the Rhine to invade German-held territory. They practiced swimming through gunfire and removing their backpacks quickly when thrown into the water.

They were young, brash, and confident, and they could hardly wait to get into action. As the day approached when they were called into battle, Reginald came down with a high fever and was put into a Dutch hospital for treatment. After all his training, he couldn't believe that he was going to be left behind. The troops went out in their boat to bravely cross the Rhine, but when they were in the middle of the river, their boat was blown up. There was no time to shed the packs and swim; they all sank and drowned.

Reginald told this story as we stood on the banks of the Rhine in Arnhem at the very spot where his friends had been killed. Tears filled his eyes as he recalled, "I lay on that bed and said, 'Thank You, God, for sparing my life. I'll give it back to You and do whatever You want me to do.'"

Somehow our cruise on the Rhine that day was more serious and spiritual than we had expected it to be. As we looked into the water that had engulfed Reginald's friends, he said, "I'm the only one God saved."

Although the troops Reginald had trained with had drowned in their Red Sea, Reginald had been passed over, spared, and saved to give his testimony to others.

SECTION THREE

Arriving at the Destination

LESSON 12

Leave Egypt —
And Follow the Cloud

Read Exodus 16–19.

As I travel around to different places, people often give me souvenirs of their city. I have collected such diverse mementos as a wooden cutting board carved in the shape of Texas, a gallon of home-grown honey from the Rio Grande Valley, special pralines from Louisiana, hand-crafted silver jewelry from New Mexico, and a blue Delft plate from Amsterdam. I've been given so many luscious fruit baskets that at the end of one long trip, I got on the plane with two baskets of goodies hanging on each arm, looking like little Red Riding Hood!

What have you and I collected so far on our journey to Jesus? Did you bring back an apple from the Garden of Eden, a map of Enoch's 300-year walk with God, a wooden replica of Noah's ark, complete with pairs of little animals? Did you purchase a miniature pillar of salt, a replica of the ram in the thicket, a statue of Abraham, or a bottle of water from Rebekah's well? Or have you been collecting more eternal "mementos" — times of refreshing spent in the presence of the Lord?

What have you gathered up so far? Our trip should not be without memories, without pictures of those we've met, without recollections of the steps we've taken, the mountains we've climbed, the lessons we've learned. But our trip isn't over yet. We don't need to look for God on the plain, in the rain, on a walk, or on a rock. We can meet Him face to face! Let's prepare ourselves now for the most exciting part of our journey.

We will follow the same plan God gave to Moses, we will make the same moves the Hebrews made when they left the slavery of Egypt and headed for the Promised Land. They had to make a choice. Let's start with their Passover decision.

For God's People in Bible Times

Before God could catch the full attention of His people, He had to take them out of Egypt, an idolatrous country where they were slaves, where little was asked of them spiritually. The book of Hebrews tells us that...

> *...by faith Moses, when he had grown up, refused to be known as the son of Pharaoh's daughter. He chose to be mistreated along with the people of God rather than to enjoy the pleasures of sin for a short time.... By faith he left Egypt, not fearing the king's anger; he persevered because he saw him who is invisible.*
>
> —Hebrews 11:24–25, 27

Moses *knew* the invisible God who appeared in the form of a burning bush to send him back to Egypt to save the people. At first, Moses seemed to be a hero who had come to rescue the Hebrews from 400 years of slavery. But when God sent the plagues as demonstrations of His power to Pharaoh, there were many who weren't sure they really wanted to leave Egypt. They knew *of* God, but they didn't *know* God, and so they had little faith to call upon. The night on which God was to "pass over" each Hebrew home and spare the children became a moment of decision. Would they do what Moses had said to do? What guarantee would there be that they would escape Pharaoh's wrath? Did this Promised Land that the God of Moses offered those with faith actually exist? Each family had to decide that night whether to take a chance on God and move on toward the land of promise — or stay in Egypt, the land of familiarity.

When you haven't practiced the presence of God in your life, when you haven't walked and talked with Him in the garden, it's not easy to take that step of faith.

> *When our fathers were in Egypt,*
> *they gave no thought to your miracles;*
> *they did not remember your many kindnesses,*
> *and they rebelled by the sea, the Red Sea.*
>
> —Psalm 106:7

For those who made the right decision, the Exodus was not an easy trip, but God met their every need and provided miracles along the way for encouragement. Those who obeyed His instructions were blessed because they were willing to *leave Egypt* and give God a chance.

For Us in Today's World

What does the Exodus mean to you and me today? Is there some "Egypt" that you are unwilling to leave behind? What is it? Are you close enough to God to trust Him for tomorrow? This is the first step in finding peace: being willing to leave Egypt and trust God, being willing to leave the known for the unknown — in faith.

The writer of Hebrews had the benefit of hindsight when he said of Moses: *He regarded disgrace for the sake of Christ as of greater value than the treasures of Egypt, because he was looking ahead to his reward* (Hebrews 11:26).

What treasures of Egypt can't you bear to leave behind? Would you rather take your basket of souvenirs and go home? God is calling you from your present world and offering you a reward in the future. Are you willing to make a choice? To take a chance?

Perhaps until now you've been trying to get close to God but you haven't left Egypt. Perhaps you had some destructive habits that you were unwilling to give up. Perhaps you have some "secret sins" that no one knows about and you haven't been disciplined enough to change. Perhaps you're too busy with the pleasures of Egypt to spend any time with the Lord.

Put those tokens of your Egypt behind you. The Lord will bring you new joy that is better than anything Egypt has to offer.

Consulting the Map

One of the many amazing things about God is His ability to change us, to give us a renovated spiritual heart. While the world looks at Christianity from the outside, saying, "Ooh, I do not want that. I'll have to give up everything I like!" the Christian life is not about never having fun. It's about God changing us from the inside out and giving us His joy in life.

Review the following scriptures and note what each verse says about our change in desires.

Ezekiel 11:19

Romans 6:6

_____

Romans 8:4–6

_____

1 Corinthians 15:46

_____

2 Corinthians 4:16

_____

2 Corinthians 5:17

_____

Ephesians 2:10

_____

Ephesians 4:23–24

_____

Colossians 3:9–10

_____

As Christians, we can still do the things we want, but as we draw closer to God, the things we want change.

In his book _My Utmost for His Highest,_ Oswald Chambers wrote:

> God is not with our natural life while we pamper it; but when we put it out
> in the desert and resolutely keep it under, then God will be with it; and He
> will open up wells and oases, and fulfill all His promises for the natural.[1]

Is God calling you out of Egypt into the desert where He can get your attention? Is He trying to change your desires, but you're not responding? Are you fearful of what unknown place

He might send you to or what treasures and pleasures of your Egypt He might strip away? Give Him a try; make a decision, for *leaving Egypt* is the first step in finding God. He doesn't want to punish you, but to bless you: *Out of Egypt I called my son* (Matthew 2:15).

When the Israelites in Egypt made the choice to leave their homes, their shaky faith in a God whom they didn't really know needed some help. They wanted to view this God and know He was real, so God came to them in the form of a cloud that they could see.

How many of us feel that if we could witness a miracle, if we could see God part the Red Sea, if we could observe some tangible sign of His presence, *then* we would believe?

We live in a society that doesn't want to believe in anything it can't touch, eat, possess, drive, or enjoy. We are realists; what you see is what you get. We're afraid to trust people, so we don't dare have faith in God. Yet the Bible tells us *without faith it is impossible to please God, because anyone who comes to him must believe that he exists and that he rewards those who earnestly seek him* (Hebrews 11:6).

> WHAT IS FAITH? *It is the confident assurance that something we want is going to happen. It is the certainty that what we hope for is waiting for us, even though we cannot see it up ahead.*
>
> —Hebrews 11:1, TLB

Faith is the substance of things hoped for, the evidence of things not seen (Hebrews 11:1, KJV). How do we get faith? *Faith cometh by hearing, and hearing by the word of God* (Romans 10:17, KJV).

For us who haven't seen the literal parting of the Red Sea, we gain faith by studying the Word of God and reliving the times of the Old Testament heroes. The Hebrews had only to listen and obey. They had evidence of things we have not seen.

Would we really have been any different if we'd been there with Moses? Would we have experienced that certainty of God's presence if we could have heard His voice or seen Him in a cloud?

God had already put His people to the test. They had lived through the plagues, observed the Passover, and left Egypt! To reinforce their faith in Him, God chose to appear before them in the form of a cloud. He was right there for them to see. When they woke up in the morning and looked outside of their tent, there was tangible evidence that their God was alive and well. Yet their faith was still weak. The cloud that had originally so impressed them had become ordinary after a month in the wilderness. They didn't believe God, and they were sure they were going to die in the desert.

Even though their faith had been amplified by visual aids, God had to prove Himself to them over and over again. God came to them in three ways: as a cloud of defense, a cloud of dwelling, and a cloud of direction.

For Us in Today's World

Since God does not stand before us today in a visible form, where do we find our direction? Is there a godly guide for us? How grateful we should be that we have the travel plan, the roadmap — the Bible. It's God's rule book for our lives. Faith comes from hearing God's Word. Let's look together at God's direction for our spiritual vision in Psalm 121 (KJV):

I will lift up mine eyes unto the hills, from whence cometh my help.
My help cometh from the LORD, which made heaven and earth.
He will not suffer thy foot to be moved: he that keepeth thee will not slumber.
Behold, he that keepeth Israel shall neither slumber nor sleep.
The LORD is thy keeper: the LORD is thy shade upon thy right hand.
The sun shall not smite thee by day, nor the moon by night.
The LORD shall preserve thee from all evil: he shall preserve thy soul.
The LORD shall preserve thy going out and thy coming in from this time forth, and
even for evermore.

In this psalm God tells us to lift up our eyes, not to keep our heads down in discouragement and worldly disappointment. He affirms that our help and direction come from Him, the Great Creator. As He watched over Israel and was their defense, so He will keep a watchful eye over us. Although we don't see His cloud, He promises He will shade us from the heat of our daily activities and protect us from harm. As we choose to dwell in Him, He will preserve our comings and goings forevermore.

Consulting the Map

We are encouraged to look heavenward! Yet in our culture, prayer typically takes place with our heads bowed.

Read the following verses and note how each says to pray and under what circumstances.

	HOW TO PRAY	**WHY**
Exodus 2:23	_____	_____
Exodus 34:8	_____	_____
Numbers 20:6	_____	_____
1 Samuel 15:11	_____	_____
1 Kings 8:22	_____	_____
1 Kings 8:54	_____	_____
2 Chronicles 20:18	_____	_____
Psalm 95:6	_____	_____
Ecclesiastes 5:2	_____	_____
Daniel 6:10	_____	_____
Matthew 6:6	_____	_____
Matthew 26:39	_____	_____
Mark 1:35	_____	_____
Mark 6:46	_____	_____
Mark 11:25	_____	_____
Luke 5:16	_____	_____
Luke 6:12	_____	_____
Luke 22:41	_____	_____
John 17:1	_____	_____
Ephesians 3:14	_____	_____

As a reminder of what we learned in lesson 7, read Psalm 4:3. Does God hear our prayers?

_____

_____

Based on the above scripture passages, does God hear our prayers when we look up? When we bow down? When we lie down? When we stand up? When we are in public, or in private?

Do you believe God hears your prayers when you are driving, doing dishes, in bed, or at a soccer game?

"The proper way for men to pray," said Deacon Samuel Keys,

"At least the best for me is down upon the knees."

"Oh, I should say the way to pray," said Reverend Dr. Wise,

"Is standing straight with arms outstretched and rapt and upturned eyes."

"Oh, no, no, no," said Elder Slow, "that posture is too proud!"

"A man should pray with eyes fast closed, and head serenely bowed."

"I fell in Hitchkins' well the other day, head first," said Willie Brown.

"Both my feet was a stickin' up and my head was a stickin' down."

"I prayed a prayer right then and there...best prayer I ever prayed!

The prayin-ist prayer I ever said was standin' on my 'haid!"[2]

What a comfort to know that God is real and that He hears our prayers! He watches over us by day and by night; He neither slumbers nor sleeps.

As you and I take the next step in our journey to Jesus, we leave our Egypts behind and follow the cloud that leads us to a place of rest and peace. We are no longer going to sit on the fence of indecision; we are going to make the choice to follow God.

Trip Journal

1. What unusual souvenirs have you brought home in the past? How have they helped you to recall your trip?

2. What is "Egypt" to you? What habits have you already changed with God's power? What do you see in your life that still needs to be left behind or eliminated?

3. Have you ever made a difficult but necessary decision? What was it, and did you make the right choice?

4. Read Hebrews 11 in your favorite version. What is the theme that runs through these Old Testament reviews? What is your own definition of faith? Compare this with verse 1. Using your own and the Bible's definition, how would you evaluate your faith?

5. Read John 20:24–28. What was Thomas's level of faith? Do you relate to Thomas? If so, in what way? What was Jesus' attitude to him and whom did He say He would bless? How can we increase our faith?

For Your Notebook

To make God's Word become real to you, write out Psalm 121 and insert your own personal translation after each verse — first write the verse and then what it means to you. This method of Bible study is a great way of personalizing scripture so that it comes alive for you.

Scenic Overlook

Living in our family store on the town square, we had only one hill to look up to — a gradual rise behind our local church across the street. While it wasn't Mount Sinai, when we lifted up our eyes, we saw the parsonage and, in our childish minds, the place where God lived. Reverend Orville Ullom was the only God we knew. He was a kindly man who spoke softly and donned his "God-robes" on Sunday — long black gowns with velvet stripes often adorned with an assortment of what appeared to be colorful scarves. He had red velvet for Christmas, deep gold for autumn, and purple for Easter. Our God dressed up for special occasions, and when church was over, Reverend Ullom walked back up the hill from whence he came. As far as we were concerned, he ascended into the heavenlies.

Since my childhood, I've always associated lifting my eyes up to the hills with seeing God. When I look at a mountain with a big cloud covering its peak, I know that God is at home and all's well with the world.

In the early 1970s, Fred and I bought a home in the foothills of the San Bernardino mountains. The house jutted out over a deep canyon and looked onto vast hillsides that had few trees. My kitchen window faced bare mountains, and at first I thought there was no beauty in hills that produced little but mustard weed. Having grown up in New England where everything was green, I felt these stripped-down mountains looked naked.

Yet, as I watched throughout the seasons, these hills, like Reverend Ullom, changed their scarves. Winter brought a white bow of beauty as the snow nestled its way around the top of the peaks and wrapped up the crests for Christmas. As the snow melted in the spring, a green belt surrounded the hills, and by June, bright polka dots of yellow mustard weed burst forth. The scorching heat of summer then burned up the bushes which, by fall, broke off at the base and began to roll across the hills in the Santa Ana winds — tumbling tumbleweeds bounced across my backyard leaving their prints on the brown background.

In November 1970, what was called the "Big Bear Burn" raged through our hills. We looked up, transfixed as a wild wall of flames crested our hills and marched down the mountains toward our home. Hurricane winds propelled the lighted tumbleweeds like balls of flame and the olive trees burst like fireworks as each oil-laden leaf became a mini-torch against a blackened sky.

My son Fred, six years old at the time, called the family to prayer as the firemen stood with hoses poised surrounding the house. He handed me a Bible and said, "Mother, read us something that will tell us God won't let our house burn." Was God with us on the mountain that night? Was He awake and not slumbering? Would He save our home if we looked up to the hills?

God did deliver us from the forest fire flaming furiously around our home. Just as the inferno reached our deck, the winds shifted. Half of the fire went on one side of us and half went over the house and down the other side of the hill. It was our Passover. It was God parting our Red Sea. It was Moses holding up his rod for a miracle to take place. We met God face to face on our mountain that night, and He has preserved our "going out" and our "coming in" ever since. He even brought several neighbors to Himself that night — one teenager prayed to receive the Lord while he was holding a hose on our roof.

When the fire had passed over us, we found one charred post that God had left as a reminder of the reality of the flames, lest we forget. Later, I hung a little plaque at the front door for each visitor to read and for me to see each day. It was that verse I'd loved as a child, but with new meaning for me and my family.

I will lift up mine eyes unto the hills, from whence cometh my help.

My help cometh from the LORD, which made heaven and earth.

—Psalm 121:1–2, KJV

Don't wait until the fire comes before you look for God. He's on the mountain waiting for you right now. He's holding out the roadmap that will lead you back to Him. Take it in your hand and follow it.

LESSON 13

Listen to God — And Obey His Commands

Read Exodus 20–24.

One summer when I was speaking at a Bible conference in Lake Okaboji, Iowa, an elderly and sprightly gentleman gave the evening message on the Ten Commandments. On a table before him were ten tall vases of different shapes and colors. He explained that these would represent the Ten Commandments as he taught them. He then told the story of a person who knew what he should have done in life but didn't actually do it. When the little man told about the first violation, he picked up a huge mallet and whacked the first vase with every ounce of strength he had. The thing smashed instantly and pieces flew out into the audience. Everyone screamed in surprise. If there were any dozing souls in the audience, there weren't anymore. Each person was sitting up straight and alert, awaiting the other nine commandments. As the man would say, "And he broke the third commandment," he would break another vase and the audience would duck and cover their faces. There may have been better speakers that summer, but I can't remember them. However, I will never forget the man with the mallet, merrily breaking the Ten Commandments.

When he was finished, a pastor near me told me that this same gentleman had spoken at his church. In the morning service, he had asked the ladies of the church to bring vases he could use in his evening message. He obviously had not communicated what he was going to do with the vases because in true female style, they all brought lovely items, representative of their families, worthy of display in front of the entire congregation. You can imagine the response as the man raised his mallet and smashed the first vase! The pastor said nine ladies rose from their seats, ran up the aisle, and grabbed their vases off the table, while the first lady whose vase was destroyed sat shocked and sobbed out loud. The whole program stopped, and the group sang hymns while the elders searched the church basement for old vases, knowing that the show must go on. I'm sure no one in that church will ever forget the breaking of the Ten Commandments!

How about you? Is there any nagging sense of guilt about any of these commandments that has stayed in your mind over the years? God has always been a God of order, and He expects us to obey His clear instructions. God gave us His commandments, not that He expected any one of us to be perfect, but so we would have an ultimate standard by which to judge our own behavior. When we set rules for our children, we know they won't happily do everything we want, but they will know their limits.

In our present society, we have rebelled against many restrictions, and we have cried out for our rights. We want to be free to "do our own thing." Yet, even the most liberal thinker would have to agree that our moral standards have disintegrated as we have loudly proclaimed, "If it feels good, do it!"

For God to give us rules almost seems old-fashioned. Rules were something that we were forced to obey as children, but now that we are mature, we like to think they have become obsolete. We want to enjoy the "good life" without guilt or care. Some of us remember a pastor who taught us rules in such a heavy manner that we were sure the Christian life contained nothing but "don'ts." Some of us may picture Moses as we saw him in our Sunday school books — a stern, unloving old man in a white dress, holding what appeared to be two tombstones. Some of us may see him as Charlton Heston, his rich voice rolling out the Ten Commandments like poetry. Whatever our preconceived notions of Moses are, we must remember that he was the man God chose to save His people.

Consulting the Map

Read the following scriptures and in your own words, note the general content of each and respond to the question at the end.

Exodus 34:28

_____

_____

Deuteronomy 4:13

_____

_____

Deuteronomy 5:6–21

_____

_____

Deuteronomy 10:4

_____

_____

As we have seen so far in our study of the Old Testament, the nation of Israel is often likened to children. Think of your own parenting experience (even if it is as an aunt, uncle, or babysitter). When God gave ten clear commandments, why do you think He repeated them, or made reference to them so often?

_____

_____

_____

_____

These rules had actually been part of Jewish culture before Mount Sinai, but Moses' presentation gave them divine endorsement.

Let's listen to what God has to say — and try not to break any vases!

1. Worship no other God (Exodus 20:3).

The word _worship_ means to honor, to revere, or to pay respect. In contrast to other cultures who had gods for every season and for all manners of reasons, our God made it clear right from the beginning that He is the one and only God and that He alone is to be worshiped. The believing Hebrew was to stay true to Jehovah; the Creator; the Great I AM; the Father of Abraham, Isaac, and Jacob; the One who brought them out of Egypt; the Lord God. If we wish to know God personally, we must first establish Him as the only object worthy of worship, and fall down before Him in a spirit of reverence. How much time do we spend praising God for who He is? A great way to get acquainted with God is to start calling out to Him in honor and in worship and to listen when He answers. We won't be able to resist the Great I AM.

Consulting the Map

Because our culture is not one in which we are accustomed to physical idols or thinking of "a thing" as a god, the idea of worshiping another god may seem foreign to us. To understand what meaning this might have for us today, let's first look at what worship is.

Worship can mean different things to different people, but however we choose to worship God, it is always in response to His holy presence. Look up the following verses, and note the selected attributes of God that make Him worthy of reverence.

Deuteronomy 4:31

_____

Psalm 18:35; Isaiah 40:11

_____

Psalm 97:9

_____

Isaiah 42:5

_____

Jeremiah 33:11

_____

Revelation 4:11

_____

In the space provided, write down your personal experience with these attributes of God and how they bring you to worship Him.

_____

_____

_____

_____

_____

2. Don't bow to images or idols (Exodus 20:4).

In our society today, we are not accustomed to the idea of "other gods." The Hebrew people, however, fresh out of 400 years in a land of idolatry and heading for the Promised Land that was populated by Baal worshipers, needed to be warned against bowing down to pagan images.

Do we still need to heed this rule today? Have you ever put faith in statues, plaques, relics, saints, or visions? Have you worshiped wealth, position, big homes, wall-to-wall carpeting, or a lovely decor? Do you idolize parents, pastors, children, or celebrities? Have you ever been addicted to drugs, alcohol, food, or gambling?

When we put our focus on any activity, person, thing, or compulsion to such a degree that we are worshiping it — being mentally consumed by it — we are bowing before something other than God. We may not be creating a literal golden calf, but we are not practicing the presence of God, a God who is jealous of our time and attention — not because He wants to "rain on our parade," but because He knows that the deepest longing of the human heart is a relationship with Him. Just because our culture has chosen to ignore many of God's laws does not mean that He has removed the rules or the retribution. His laws are for our lives, for our own good, and as a Father, He will reward those who obey.

Consulting the Map

Earlier we looked at worshiping God. Now we turn to what idols mean to our Christian life today. *The International Standard Bible Encyclopedia* explains it this way:

> Idolatry originally meant the worship of idols, or the worship of false gods by means of idols, but came to mean among the Old Testament Hebrews any worship of false gods, whether by images or otherwise, and finally the worship of Yahweh through visible symbols and ultimately in the New Testament idolatry came to mean, not only the giving to any creature or human creation the honor or devotion which belonged to God alone, but the giving to any human desire a precedence over God's will.[1]

For our purposes, let's focus on the last part of the definition: "the giving to any human desire a precedence over God's will." Think about some of the things in your life that may have taken precedence over God's will. A few ideas to jumpstart your thinking might be career success, popularity, marriage, children, entertainment, or possessions.

List those items here.

_____

_____

Read Habakkuk 2:19 and note what good an idol is.

_____

_____

Read the following verses and note what we should do with idols and why.

	WHAT WE SHOULD DO	THE REASON WHY
Joshua 24:14	_____	_____
1 Samuel 7:3	_____	_____
2 Kings 23:24	_____	_____

Write a prayer to the Lord asking Him to help you remove from your life the specific idols you listed above. Ask for His help to serve Him faithfully with your whole heart, in order to keep the second commandment.

_____

_____

_____

_____

_____

3. Don't use God's name irreverently (Exodus 20:7).

God's name is never to be used as a swear word, and how quickly we must explain to our children the seriousness of taking the Lord's name in vain. Don't simply tell them not to do it, but show them that they are hurting God, their Creator, when they do so. Don't let them watch TV programs where the "good guys" use God's name in vain as if it were a sign of manliness.

I once went to a movie for the sole purpose of seeing my brother Ron who had a role in it. Right from the beginning the main characters were swearing, and I would have left except that I hadn't seen Ron's part yet. Upsetting as the profanity was at first to me, after an hour of it, I was hardly hearing it. What this experience showed me was that if you listen to something offensive long enough, it loses its shock value. If any of us watch or listen to anything we know we shouldn't, we will become somewhat accepting of it sooner or later.

A relatively new addition to our radio programs is what's called a "shock jock." Do you have one in your listening area? These entertainers use filthy language and treat bizarre sexual behavior as the norm. Are you, your mate, or your children listening to such programs as amusement? This commandment doesn't just address speaking God's name in vain, but it also applies to listening to any type of perversion in an accepting way.

4. Observe the Sabbath as a holy day of rest (Exodus 20:8).

Because God created the world in six days and then rested on the seventh, He commands us to do the same. Work is a necessity of life, but God wants us to rest from our pursuits one day each week and worship Him. I remember how important our day of rest was when I was a child. There was never a question of whether we felt like going to church or whether it was convenient; we all got ready and went. Worshiping the Lord came first without question. After church we had our biggest meal of the week; it was a time of celebration. In the evening, my mother would lead us into our little den behind the store, where I would play the piano, Ron the trumpet, and Mother the violin. Jim would lead the singing, and Father would stand in the doorway "keeping an eye on the store." From my childhood I have learned to keep the Lord's Day holy!

Consulting the Map

Trying to understand the fourth commandment may bring some questions to your mind, like which day is the Sabbath: Saturday or Sunday? And why does modern evangelical Christianity seem to ignore this particular commandment? Let's consult the map and see what else God's Word has to say about this matter.

Read the following verses and note your observations about the Sabbath, the law, and Christians meeting together. (Hint: Reading several translations may help here.)

Matthew 22:36–40

_____

_____

Mark 2:27

_____

_____

Luke 13:10–17

_____

_____

John 5:1–18

_____

_____

Galatians 3:23–25

_____

_____

Hebrews 10:25

_____

_____

According to what you read here, is God more concerned with the letter of the law, or the _intent_ of the law?

_____

Based on these scriptures, write out your personal commitment to keeping the Sabbath.

_____

_____

What changes will you make to your current practices based on these verses?

_____

_____

5. Honor your father and mother (Exodus 20:12).

As I grew up, it never occurred to me or any of my friends to be rude or disrespectful to our parents, but this commandment needs to be brought out of the archives and freshened up for today's youth who seem to have never heard it. In times when courts will award children money because they don't feel their parents did the best they could in raising them, and when insecure parents have followed media suggestions to not damage their progeny by disciplining them, we have bred a generation of young people who are brash and disrespectful.

Since God commands that we honor our parents, is there any hope that we can fellowship with God and know His power if we are not showing honor to our parents? And parents, can we know God's power if we are allowing our own children to be disrespectful toward us?

I remember once when our son made some fresh comment to me in Fred's presence. Fred grabbed him quickly, picked him up off the floor, and said, "Don't ever let me hear you speak to my wife like that again!" He set the stunned child down, and I never had trouble with him from that moment on. He learned he was to honor his mother, and he is now teaching this to his own child.

My son-in-law Chuck is a marriage and family therapist. He says that one of the most common problems he sees is young boys being allowed to talk back or say bad things to their mothers. He sees this lack of respect for women as a core problem in our society and as a key source of the preponderance of violence against women. He advises his clients that when there is a problem with respect to the mother, that the father stop everything and address it on the spot — much like Fred did with our own son.

The rod of correction imparts wisdom, but a child left to himself disgraces his mother (Proverbs 29:15).

6. Don't murder (Exodus 20:13).

Although this is a rule we ourselves may not ever literally disobey, we are living in times when a high-school boy shot his teacher because she gave him a low grade. Times when a commentator reported on the impossibility of keeping guns out of the hands of elementary-school children. Times when the thinking among many people seems to be: "If you don't get your own way, shoot someone. It's your right." What a pitiful, ungodly attitude — an attitude that naturally follows when children are allowed to be disrespectful to their parents. If you have no spirit of honor for your parents and you aren't taught differently, you will have no respect for life. Couple this attitude with the amount of TV violence most children view, and it is understandable why homicide and suicide are the top causes of teenage death. Thousands of women who wouldn't kill a fly or trap a mouse seek to have legal abortions each year. One doctor was even sued for malpractice when the fetus he was aborting lived!

7. Don't commit adultery (Exodus 20:14).

This rule seems to have become old-fashioned, even "out of vogue," if the women's magazines, movies, or TV soap operas are to be believed. Married people no longer commit "adultery" — they have extramarital affairs; and the unmarried just become "sexually active." Unfortunately this is not just a problem out in the world, but it is a very real problem in the Christian church. Because God's clear statement becomes cloudy in our minds, we rationalize that "even God Himself couldn't stay faithful to this sad excuse for a mate." A radio commentator, bemoaning the epidemic of AIDS in this country, cautioned his listeners to engage in "safe sex." He then added, almost as a side note, "It's almost as if we should only have one partner." God's old rule is a new idea in America today.

One day I watched spellbound as a talk show hostess interviewed three prostitutes as if they were schoolteachers. Each told how she got into "the business" and then described a few "clients." One aggressive example even had a beeper so if her services were needed while she was out shopping, she wouldn't miss a call. When asked if she could earn her living in a nicer way, one responded, "I was a secretary and took home $180 a week, but I can earn more than that in a couple of hours so I'd be stupid to return to an office."

One of the three was religious and when asked if she thought what she did was a sin, she was shocked and quoted Jesus in her defense: "The Lord approved of prostitution," she stated, "for didn't He let the adulterous woman go, by asking those without sin to cast the first stone?" The audience responded well to this logic. They assumed that Jesus must have been a free thinker, not knowing that after He forgave the woman He said, *"Go, and sin no more"* (John 8:11, KJV).

We can always find a verse that, out of context, seems to support a pattern of loose living, but God doesn't bless adulterous relationships because it is against His clear commandment.

8. Don't steal (Exodus 20:15).

In an age when people take towels from hotels and ashtrays from restaurants, it's difficult to teach children not to steal. In times when the police are too busy with bigger crimes to respond to petty theft, ordinary people can grab what they want and many times get away with it. My son-in-law Randy has a store that sells gold coins and jewelry. It is in a large enclosed mall with a paid security staff. One day when a suspicious-looking individual was lurking around, Randy called the guard, who then reprimanded Randy for summoning him *before* anything was stolen. The suspect, who was extremely tall, left, but that evening Randy looked up to see the same man running into the store. He leaped over the counter, grabbed all the gold chains that were hanging on the far wall, jumped back over the counter, and was gone before Randy could get to the phone. There was nothing to be done. It was all over, and he had to suffer the loss.

Most of us would never do such a blatant thing, yet we will run off copies of Christian music to save our church money — and feel virtuous. We will use funny lines or good examples from books or other speakers without giving credit and hope no one happens to have read the book that week. Often, we Christians feel exempt from worldly restrictions because we're doing it "for the Lord," who, if He happens to notice our little theft, will forgive us when He sees what a blessing we've been to the budget.

9. Don't lie (Exodus 20:16).

When we recall how deception was a family trait that began with Adam and Eve and how Jacob was eventually named "the deceiver," we see how important it was for God to let His people know that lying, covering up, or misleading someone is a sin. "Don't lie," He told Moses, who delivered the word to the people. God feels that telling the truth is important, and teaching our children to be honest is a necessity if we wish them to become adults who are pleasing to the Lord.

Honesty is a very difficult principle to teach if we're not living it ourselves. If a child tells you who is on the phone and you say, "Tell her I'm not home," you are lying and teaching your child to lie also. If you brag about what you got away with in filing your taxes, or say one thing about a friend behind her back and another thing to her face, you are being dishonest.

Paul said to the Ephesians, *"No more lying, then! Everyone must tell the truth to his fellow believer, because we are all members together in the body of Christ"* (Ephesians 4:25, TEV).

10. Don't covet (Exodus 20:17).

For those of you who may have been perfect on the first nine commandments perhaps even you may have a problem with number ten! We are told not to desire, long for, or crave something (anything) that belongs to someone else. When I first read this commandment with meaning, I realized that I coveted everything I saw. I wanted it all! Coming from a childhood without curtains or even a scatter rug on the floor, I longed for drapes and carpeting. I could rationalize that I deserved them, especially if *someone else* had them. Even though I know better, if I come to visit you today and you have new monogrammed towels, I'll want them.

God knew where to catch us when He told us not to be envious of other people's houses and possessions. He told us not to wish we were married to the man next door. The grass is always greener, but there may be no roots. We are not even to be envious of the cleaning lady or the boy who cuts our neighbor's lawn, or the neighbor who has a poodle or a Siamese cat, or a Mazda or Mercedes. We shouldn't covet anything that belongs to our neighbor.

Coveting is such a subtle sin that most of us don't confess it or even dignify it with a plea for forgiveness; yet wishing we had more than we have is a sin of great significance to God, although we sometimes misname it as "goal-setting," especially when the desire is to possess what our neighbor has.

Consulting the Map

The *Random House Webster's Unabridged Dictionary* defines being covetous as "inordinately or wrongly desirous of wealth or possessions; greedy."[2]

Read the following two scripture passages and note what covetousness, or greed, is likened to.

Ephesians 5:3–5

_____

Colossians 3:5

_____

Do you remember the second commandment? What does it say about false gods?

_____

_____

Are these rules, given to Moses by God so long ago, of any significance to us today? Is the order in which they were given of any importance? As I have studied them and applied them to America today, I think they give an explanation to an otherwise unexplainable society.

Keeping in mind the commandments we've just reviewed, let's look at how quickly a whole nation can go downhill when those rules are forgotten — when we abandon God.

1. Our country was founded on biblical principles and the desire for freedom from religious persecution. Our leaders were godly men, our government was based on the Judeo-Christian ethic, and our colleges had religious affiliations. The phrase "in God we trust" was printed on our money, church attendance was an accepted way of life, and those who violated the laws were punished. We were a nation who worshiped God.

2. Our reputation was important, and our families were the foundation of our culture. But in the 1900s things began to change. With advances in modern science, God no longer seemed relevant, and church attendance declined. On April 8, 1966, *Time* magazine declared on its cover "God Is Dead," and slowly people began to believe it. Young people strayed into strange cults, and flower children wilted on street corners.

3. Because there were doubts about the existence of God, taking His name in vain hardly mattered. Crude language became acceptable and later, even a sign of masculinity or self-importance.

4. When you're not even sure there is a God, going to church seems unnecessary. Leave it to the older people who aren't quite "with it," or to those who are weak and need a crutch. Why not take the whole weekend off now that we have no obligations? Why not use those days to pursue pleasure and give ourselves some of the fun we never had when we were forced to go to church?

5. If you don't have much honor for God, then why respect your parents? You didn't ask to be born, and most of your problems are their fault. They're both working so hard to get enough money to buy all the things they covet, that they're never around anyway. As one young girl said to me, "I end up being responsible for my little brother and for getting dinner. That shouldn't be my job. I have rights, you know."

6. When you spend a lot of time watching TV, it's not hard to get ideas you might not have thought of alone — stabbing, shooting, drugging, drinking, molesting, or maybe even murder. These are often used by characters on TV as solutions to their problems. If there isn't a God, there's no heaven or hell, so you might as well live it up while you're here.

7. Some have decided it's time now to throw out old Victorian abstinence and religious morals that have damaged our psyches and kept us inhibited. We've been held down too long by our old beliefs — let's loosen up and have some fun. If religion is just a list of don'ts, let's do them. Let's eat, drink, shoot up, and experiment with sex, for tomorrow we may die — whatever that means.

8. If God is no longer looking at our lives, what difference does it make if we take something that's not ours or if we cheat on our exams or our income tax — as long as we don't get caught?

9. When there's no standard for truth, no yardstick of honesty left, then there's no black and white; all becomes gray and anything goes. Deception becomes a close friend.

10. Now that we're no longer hung up on rules, we can spend our time freely doing the things that make us happy, without any restrictions or guilty conscience. We can buy all those items we've been coveting for years, and won't the neighbors be jealous! We can lust after a different mate a week and not feel guilty.

Isn't it amazing that when we remove God, consider Him dead, and seek our own ways, morals and human decency come tumbling down soon after?

What need is there for the Ten Commandments today? Paul said the Law *was added in order to show what wrongdoing is* (Galatians 3:19, TEV). *The law was our schoolmaster to bring us unto Christ* (Galatians 3:24, KJV).

If we have no tape measure, we don't know how far away we've strayed. Recently, reports have been made that the only way to curb teenage pregnancy, abortions, and illegitimate births is to provide birth-control clinics on high-school campuses to dispense information and contraceptives, even without parental permission. I was literally stopped in my tracks one afternoon when I turned on the TV just in time to hear the afternoon talk-show host ask a crowd of teenagers on spring break in Fort Lauderdale if it was true that the hotels were putting free condoms in the same drawers with the Gideon Bibles. As I stared in disbelief, the boys cheerfully waved the evidence before the cameras.

A new opinion, crying out like John the Baptist in the wilderness, is "Just Say No." You don't have to make love to every guy who passes your way. You don't have to have herpes to be happy. At the pharmacy counter, I recently saw a display of "Just Say No" buttons for $1.98 apiece. I wonder if they'll catch on.

This startling proposal of abstinence has been received with high humor by the press who consider it too much of a long shot to be worth a second thought. "Rules for the teens? Ridiculous!"

One commentator on TV said, "The sexual revolution has gone too far to think a few 'no's' in the crowd would make much difference." Another added, "There's no point in making rules when you know no one will obey them."

One morning on the *Today* show, Dr. Art Ulene gave a surprising plea for abstinence outside of marriage. He gave facts and figures of current problems and said there's no such thing as "safe sex." The interviewer asked, "Aren't you being a bit unrealistic to think the kids will say no?" The doctor won my respect when he said, "We don't eliminate morals because people don't obey the rules. I tell my kids what's right, and if they get in trouble, it's not because I didn't warn them."

If you've been looking for God in a few wrong places, perhaps you should review the commandments and see if you've been playing in the gray area — perhaps what you're doing is not *too* bad but not quite in line with God's laws. With God, it's "all or nothing at all." Half of your heart isn't enough for Him.

You might say, "I could never be good enough for God. If He's looking for perfection, I'm not the one." That's probably exactly the way the Israelites felt when they saw God descend on Mount Sinai. When Moses received the Commandments from God, He came out from the cloud that hid Him. The people had seen the lightning and the smoke, and had heard the thunder and the trumpet blast, and they were afraid. I'm sure they were feeling insecure and wondering if they could ever be good enough for God. How did Moses calm them? He said, *"Don't be afraid … for God has come in this way to show you his awesome power, so that from now on you will be afraid to sin against him!"* (Exodus 20:20, TLB).

Not *afraid of Him* but, knowing His power, *afraid to disobey Him*. If you've been waiting until you are perfect to try to follow God's map, come to Him today just as you are, and He will bless you. Listen to what He has to say to you. God speaks to us through His Word, through our prayers, and through our minds as we quiet them before Him. Listen to God and obey His commandments.

Trip Journal

1. Why did God give us commandments that He knew few people could ever obey? What is your opinion of rules? What do you feel about the modern thought that anything is all right as long as it doesn't hurt anyone else?

2. What is your understanding of worship? How could the worship service at your church be brought closer to what God desires of His people?

3. What idols do you have in your life? What is the difference between an idol and a role model? When do things like alcohol, drugs, eating, and gambling become idols?

4. Has swearing ever been a problem in your life? If so, how did it come to your attention and what steps did you take to overcome the habit?

5. What do you remember about Sundays as a child? Was church attendance expected? Was dinner special? In your present situation, is Sunday different from any other day? In what way?

6. How were you taught to honor your father and mother? How was this method effective or ineffective in its results? What is your definition of discipline? Using a concordance, find out what God's Word says about discipline, training, and punishment.

7. What is your view on capital punishment? What does the Bible say? (See Exodus 21:12, 14.) What do you feel has caused the increase of murders and violence in this country? What can be done to change this direction? How do you feel TV influences young people in their behavior?

8. Name some TV shows in which "free sex" is a normal part of the program. What does watching soap operas do to an impressionable young mind? Are you aware that more than 50 percent of teen pregnancies are conceived in the bedroom of one of the participants, in the afternoon while watching love scenes on TV? What do you feel about talk shows on which prostitutes, homosexuals, and live-in companions are interviewed as average U.S. citizens? What do you feel the church should do when learning of an adulterous situation among their membership? What does Leviticus 20:10–24 say about sexual violations of God's laws?

9. What is the connection between the drug culture and the rise in thefts? If you found a stolen item in your child's room, what would you do about it? Have you ever taken things from hotels or restaurants that you felt you deserved? What were they and how do you feel about it now?

10. What lie can you remember telling as a child? What was done about it? Why do you feel the issues of disobedience and deception are so prominent in the Bible? How do you handle these two problems when they arise in your home?

11. What was the most recent item you coveted? What intangible thing, such as prestige or honor, have you wanted that someone else received? How are selfishness and covetousness related? What did Paul mean when he wrote, *Greed is a form of idolatry* (Colossians 3:5, TEV)?

12. What new perspective have you gained on the Ten Commandments from this study?

For Your Notebook

Start a list of tens. Ten is the number of law and government.

God gave us Ten Commandments.

Start a list of twelves. Twelve is the number of divine order.

Ishmael was the father of twelve Arab tribes.

Jacob was the father of twelve Hebrew tribes.

God gave us twelve months to organize our year.

Jesus chose twelve men for His disciples.

Make a Home for God — And Visit Him Often

Read Exodus 25–40.

As we travel along with the Israelites, we have left Egypt and followed the cloud of God's presence — comforted in the thought that He is our defense, our dwelling place, our source of direction. We have witnessed the miracle of the Red Sea's parting so that we could walk across on dry ground. We have watched Moses disappear into a cloud as he went to meet with God, and we have watched him return with the Ten Commandments. Now that we have left Egypt to follow God, now that we have listened to His voice and reviewed His laws, what's our next step?

We must do more than observe, more than trust and obey; we must make a home for God and visit Him often.

For God's People in Bible Times

After the Israelites had received the Ten Commandments, they were momentarily impressed with God. *"The LORD said to Moses, 'I am going to come to you in a dense cloud, so that the people will hear me speaking with you and will always put their trust in you'"* (Exodus 19:9). *"On the morning of the third day there was thunder and lightning, with a thick cloud over the mountain, and a very loud trumpet blast"* (Exodus 19:16).

God got their attention with His clouds, His voice, thunder and lightning, and a loud blast on the trumpet!

Consulting the Map

Before God could give His people instructions, He first had to get their attention. He did this by using thunder and lightning that proceeded from a deep, dark, and dismal electric cloud.

According to Exodus 19:19, the blare of the sounding trumpet grew louder and louder — it is thought to be similar to the trumpet that will sound proclaiming Christ's return.

God had their attention! Read Exodus 19:16 and note the people's response.

_____

_____

_____

_____

According to Hebrews 12:21, what was Moses' response?

_____

_____

_____

Read the following scriptures and note a few of the ways God used to get His people's attention, what was achieved as a result, and the purpose behind His actions.

	PERSON/S INVOLVED	ACTION	RESULT	PURPOSE
Exodus 11:1; 12:29–30	_____	_____	_____	_____
Numbers 22:1–31	_____	_____	_____	_____
2 Kings 17:9–23	_____	_____	_____	_____
Daniel 3:13–30	_____	_____	_____	_____
Daniel 6:14–27	_____	_____	_____	_____
Acts 9:1–20	_____	_____	_____	_____

God desires our complete attention. What methods has God used to get your attention?

_____

_____

_____

Sometimes His methods of getting our attention are not pleasant. According to Judges 2:14–15, how did God get His people's attention after they left Him to follow the ways of the world?

_____

_____

According to Deuteronomy 8:5, what is one of the methods God uses to get the attention of those He loves who are walking in disobedience? Does this comfort you? Why or why not?

_____

_____

_____

_____

How does Deuteronomy 8:6 say we can avoid God's needing to get our attention in this way?

_____

_____

Rewrite Deuteronomy 8:7–9 in your own words, explaining God's purpose in getting our attention.

_____

_____

_____

_____

_____

Rest Stop

God wants the best for His people, and He wants them to hear what He has to say. Are you willing to pray that God will do whatever He needs to do in order to get your attention? If so, write your prayer below, and take time to pray right now.

_____

_____

_____

_____

_____

_____

When Moses came down and read the rules to the crowds, they answered in unison, "We will obey them all!" To celebrate their obedience, Moses built a simple altar and surrounded it with twelve pillars, one for each tribe of Israel. He took the blood from the sacrificial animals

— half he poured on the altar and half he splashed toward the people saying, *"This blood confirms and seals the covenant the LORD has made with you in giving you these laws"* (Exodus 24:8, TLB).

As the Hebrew people watched Moses go up to God on the mountain, they were overwhelmed with the sight. *"Under his feet there seemed to be a pavement of brilliant sapphire stones, as clear as the heavens"* (Exodus 24:10, TLB). *"Those at the bottom of the mountain saw the awesome sight: the glory of the LORD on the mountain top looked like a raging fire"* (Exodus 24:17, TLB).

The people had received the Ten Commandments from the mountaintop; they had learned to lift up their eyes unto the hills from whence would come their help.

Then Moses disappeared one more time into the cloud on top of Mount Sinai and was there for forty days and nights while God gave him new instructions.

Until this point, the people in the Old Testament had been looking for God in all kinds of places, but finally God told Moses that He wanted him to build a home — a heaven on earth — so that God might live among His people and they would know specifically where to find Him.

In spite of the obvious evidence of God's presence, not all of the Hebrew people believed that God was real, and some even looked back with fond memories on the good ol' days in Egypt when they worshiped idols they could see. For the first time in history, God decided to come down from on high and settle with His people, His chosen race. He told Moses on the mountaintop, *"I want the people of Israel to make me a sacred Temple where I can live among them. This home of mine shall be a tent pavilion — a Tabernacle. I will give you a drawing of the construction plan, and the details of each furnishing"* (Exodus 25:8–9, TLB).

For forty days Moses listened to the instructions for building God's home on earth. Had I been Moses, I would have been flattered to be selected as the builder. Instantly I would have pictured a grandiose palace with enough wings on it to fly away. My plans would include high walls for security, a drawbridge over the moat, and a huge gate of heavy wrought iron. The mailbox would be atop a stone pillar, and on it, in simple Hebrew script, would be painted one word: GOD. I can see it all now. "Knock, knock. Is the Lord at home?"

If you were to design a house for God, what would come to your mind? Perhaps a Southern plantation with columns out front? A castle with turrets, a formidable fortress, a secluded monastery? Or would you be more spiritual and sketch out a fluffy, ethereal haven in the heavenlies, with Saint Peter at the golden gate surrounded by cheery cherubim?

If God called you to a mountaintop experience and said, "Child of mine, I'm going to come and live with you," what would your reaction be? "Who me? Surely You must be speaking to someone else. You haven't seen my house. It's just not big enough for You. There's not even a guest room, and we couldn't put God in the basement!"

Would you perhaps react in the same way you might if your mother-in-law decided to move in? Or if your mate invited the new pastor to stay with you until his home was ready? Or if Billy Graham and the Pope chose your house for their first ecumenical meeting for a TV mini-series, "Communion with the Simple Folk of America"?

When Moses asked the Lord where He intended to live, God replied, "*You* are going to build Me a home." How surprised would you have been? Where would you have chosen to build it? As I think of the possibilities, I recall a large lot I've had my eye on for years. It's on top of a rolling hill in Redlands, California, with a 360-degree view of the surrounding orange groves, bordered by tall palm trees, the desert valleys below, and the majestic snow-capped mountains. The city of Palm Springs sprawls out on one side and the natural formation of an arrowhead points to the healing mineral baths of Arrowhead Springs on the other. *I'd* like to build a house there, so I know *God* would just love it! Trees, deserts, mountains, cities, and springs — what more could He want?

"You don't want a house — You want a *tabernacle*? Well, that puts a whole new slant on it, because this lot isn't zoned for churches. But there's a beautiful spot by the freeway that's already been approved by the city for a Christian school that couldn't raise the money. Would that be a good place for Your tabernacle, God? It has easy freeway access, and it's on the right side of town."

If I'd been Moses, that's probably how I would have talked with God. I always want to be helpful and give creative suggestions, but God wasn't asking for help, and He already is the great Creator. All He wanted was a willing man to follow His clear instructions. He didn't want some structure similar to the Mormon Tabernacle in Salt Lake City, or the Crystal

Cathedral in California, or even St. Peter's Basilica in Rome. *I* would have chosen one of them, but all *He* asked for was a tent — a very special tent.

"Be sure that everything you make follows the pattern I am showing you here on the mountain" (Exodus 25:40, TLB). God was clearly saying to Moses, "Don't get creative. I have the blueprints. Just do as I say."

The Hebrews had spent years making bricks in Egypt, but God had other materials in mind. In brief, God's instructions were to:

• MAKE THE TABERNACLE-TENT *from ten colored sheets of fine-twined linen, forty-two feet long and six feet wide, dyed blue, purple, and scarlet, with cherubim embroidered on them* (Exodus 26:1–2, TLB).

• *Make fifty golden clasps to fasten the loops together, so that the Tabernacle, the dwelling place of God, becomes a single unit* (Exodus 26:6, TLB).

• Make the roof of eleven goat's-hair tarpaulins, each forty-five feet across and six feet wide, topped with a layer of rams' skins dyed red and a layer of goatskins (verses 7–8, 14).

• Frame the tent in acacia wood set in silver bases (see verses 15–25).

• Make two rooms: the Holy Place and the Holy of Holies, separated by a veil of blue, purple, and scarlet cloth with cherubim embroidered on it (see verses 31–33).

• Behind the veil, put the Ark of the Covenant containing the Ten Commandments. Make the lid of the Ark — the mercy seat — of pure gold, three feet long and two feet wide, with two cherubim on top facing each other (see Exodus 37:1–9).

• In the Holy Place, make a table of shewbread, a lampstand of pure gold with seven shafts, and an altar of incense. Use pure olive oil in the lamps and keep them burning continually, forever (see Exodus 26:35; 27:20).

• In front of the tent, place the laver of washing made from bronze mirrors and the altar of sacrifice made of acacia wood and bronze with a horn at each corner (see Exodus 27:1–8; 38:1–8).

• Surround the tent and courtyard with white linen curtain walls 150 feet long, 75 feet wide, and seven feet high (see Exodus 27:9–18).

• Make one gate in the fence and cover it with a colored embroidered curtain attached by silver hooks onto posts embedded in bronze bases (see Exodus 27:16–17; 38:18–19).

From this abbreviated version of God's instructions we can see that He was very specific in measurements and materials. He left nothing to chance. He combined bright colors with drab goatskins. He desired bronze fittings in the courtyard, silver in the Holy Place, and gold in the Holy of Holies. God cares about quality and details. As an added challenge, God told Moses to make the whole tabernacle and its fittings portable so that it could be carried throughout the wilderness and set up whenever they settled down.

Unfortunately, while Moses was on the mountaintop meditating with God in the cloud, his brother, Aaron, was having a party. He and his friends had made a golden calf to worship. They had forgotten God that quickly. Out of sight, out of mind, and the people were led astray. When Moses came down and saw what was going on, he threw down the tablets on which God Himself had written and called Aaron to task. *"What in the world did the people do to you...to make you bring such a terrible sin upon them?"* (Exodus 32:21, TLB).

Aaron, shocked at being caught in the act, recovered quickly and replied, *"Don't get so upset"* (verse 22, TLB). The King James Version provides a more dignified response: *"Let not the anger of my lord wax hot!"* In other words, "Cool it, Moses!" Then, in a sudden shift of blame, Aaron provides his alibi: *"You know these people and what a wicked bunch they are"* (Exodus 32:22, TLB). *"They are set on mischief"* (KJV). Since you were gone so long, Moses, they said to me, *"Make us a god to lead us, for something has happened to this fellow Moses who led us out of Egypt"* (Exodus 32:23, TLB). While the cat's away, the mice will play.

I'm sure that many pastors today must feel as Moses did. Can't you just hear them? "What's the use? They listen to me on Sunday. They seem to care; they thank me for my message. They say, 'Bless you, brother. Praise the Lord!' and the minute they're out of my sight, they do whatever they please. Where are You, God? Have You forsaken me?"

Aaron explained creatively how he had asked the women to bring their gold jewelry for some sort of a party game, not dreaming of how much they would bring. To maintain his detachment from the blame, he told how he just threw the gold into the fire and out came a calf. "It's surely not my fault!"

When my grandson Jonathan was five years old, he dropped a Christmas ornament, and as it smashed on the tile floor, he quickly quipped, "It's not *my* fault! It just broke automatically."

Consulting the Map

Trying to pass the blame or make excuses for sin isn't anything new; it began with the first human beings. Like Aaron, Adam cast the blame of his sin onto others.

According to Genesis 3:12, who were they and what did they do?

1. _____

2. _____

According to Genesis 3:13, who did Eve blame for her sin? What was her excuse?

_____

According to Ezekiel 18:20, where should we place the blame for our sin?

_____

Describe a time when you have placed the blame for your sin on someone else.

_____

_____

_____

_____

God instructed Adam and Eve not to eat of the fruit, but they knowingly disobeyed Him. Aaron had seen God's glory on the mountain — he also knew better.

How does Romans 1:18–20 describe those who have received the knowledge of God but remain in their sin?

_____

_____

From the time we're tiny, we know to run from responsibility and blame. For a child, this avoidance is understandable, but for Aaron? For you? For me? O Lord, help us to grow up and be able to say, "It's my fault, and I'm sorry."

God punished His children for their disobedience in worshiping an idol, and He purged the camp of all who were not on the "Lord's side." Moses took two stone tablets and went up Mount Sinai again to commune with the God who defended him, dwelt with him, and directed him from the cloud: *"I am Jehovah, the merciful and gracious God ... slow to anger and rich in steadfast love and truth"* (Exodus 34:6, TLB).

God made a new contract with Moses: God would do miracles and drive out all their enemies, and the people would obey all His commandments and never compromise with the enemy; they would break down heathen idols and worship no other gods; they would not marry those from other races; and they would celebrate the Feast of Unleavened Bread, "the Passover."

When Moses came down the mountain after forty days, his face glowed from being in the presence of God. He called a meeting to explain the church building program and to lay out the blueprints before them for their vote of approval. Since the plans had been drawn up by the original Architect, the same One who designed the Garden of Eden and Noah's ark, there were no "nay" votes. Moses explained that they would volunteer their labor for six days of each week, and then rest on the seventh day and worship their God. They were to do no work on the Sabbath, under penalty of death.

Even today in Israel and elsewhere, Hasidim (pious) ultra-Orthodox Jews keep the Sabbath holy and will not let traffic through their neighborhoods on the holy day. When I was in the Jerusalem Hilton, I was shown a sign that is put up every Friday pointing to the "Shabbat Elevator" programmed to stop at every floor so that Hasidic guests would not have to "work" by pressing a single button on the Sabbath.

Moses asked those with generous hearts to bring as free-will offerings: gold, silver, and bronze; blue, purple, scarlet, and white linen cloth; tanned rams' skins and goatskins; acacia wood and olive oil; spices for oil and incense; onyx and semi-precious stones; gold jewelry and rings. People volunteered to weave, spin, embroider, and sew, and to build, carve, forge, and construct.

As the gifts were brought to Moses, he chose, by God's appointment, a man named Bezaleel as the general superintendent of the project. Soon the workmen told Moses they had enough materials for the job and that no more donations were needed. In total, the people had contributed 3,140 pounds of gold, 9,575 pounds of silver, and 7,540 pounds of bronze (see Exodus 38:24–25, 29, TLB).

Moses took God's clear instructions, inspected the work as it was being done, and did not add any clever touches of his own. Because of his obedience to every tiny detail, Moses was blessed by God and the project progressed rapidly. *On the first day of the first month, in the second year, the Tabernacle was put together* (Exodus 40:17, TLB). It was ready as the residence of God, set for Him to move in. *Then the cloud covered the Tabernacle and the glory of the Lord filled it.... The cloud rested upon the Tabernacle during the daytime, and at night there was fire in the cloud so that all the people of Israel could see it* (verses 34, 38, TLB). If the cloud did not move, they stayed until it did. This continued throughout all their wilderness wanderings.

For Us in Today's World

God's home on earth was completed, and the cloud, the sign of His presence and protection, was evident to the twelve tribes of Jacob who were encamped wide-eyed around it. The physical setting of the tabernacle surrounded by the tents of the tribes might be compared to the early New England towns in which the church was placed on the village green and the houses were built around it. The House of God was central to their daily life, and they were never far from their spiritual source of power.

Did having God so close make a difference in their daily lives? Would you behave better if God lived across the street?

After the "dwelling place" had been completed and God's symbolic cloud was in residence, what were the people to do? The excitement was over; the challenge had been met. Perhaps you've been involved at some time in a church building program of high enthusiasm, only to see the spirit drift away when the construction was completed. Having a lofty sanctuary doesn't guarantee spiritual growth. Having God live next door doesn't make much difference if you don't know how to get in to see Him or don't even try. Our Lord never leaves us stranded; He always has a plan for us where we may practice the presence of God.

In the New Testament, Paul wrote that we, the believers, are God's building and that Jesus Christ is the foundation. *"Don't you know that you yourselves are God's temple and that God's Spirit lives in you?"* (1 Corinthians 3:16).

Consulting the Map

It has always been God's desire to dwell among His people. Before Christ came, He dwelt among His people in the tabernacle. However, at that time, only the priests had direct access to God. Christ's death on the cross eliminated our separation from God; the temple was no longer needed. We became His temple because His Spirit is now able to live within all those who believe.

Read 1 Corinthians 3:16–17 and answer the following questions.

What are we cautioned not to do?

_____

_____

How does Paul describe God's temple?

_____

_____

The word *holy* comes from the Greek word meaning "sacred." Our temple should be pure, clean, and morally blameless.

Which of the following best describes your temple?

○ **Clean. He's welcome all the time.**

○ **The house looks great, just don't open any closets.**

○ **He can sit in the living room, but I'd prefer He not tour the house.**

○ **Needs a little cleaning before He comes again.**

Is Christ at home in your heart? What changes can you make so He feels welcome there?

_____

_____

_____

_____

Paul lets us know that we don't have to go out in the desert and build a tabernacle, for we ourselves are the home of God and Jesus is the cornerstone: *In him the whole building is joined together and rises to become a holy temple in the Lord. And in him you too are being built together to become a dwelling in which God lives by his Spirit* (Ephesians 2:21–22).

How exciting for us to know that we are God's building and that He lives in us. As we make a place for Him in our hearts, we must live according to His commandments and stay out of Egypt. We must make a home for Him and visit with Him often. We must listen to what He has to say as we pray.

> *I pray that out of his glorious riches he may strengthen you with power through his Spirit in your inner being, so that Christ may dwell in your hearts through faith.*
>
> —Ephesians 3:16–17

Trip Journal

1. If God asked you to build Him a tabernacle in your town, what location would you choose? What style would you select for the building? What specific features would you be sure to include? Read Hebrew 9:1–10.

2. When I talked to a friend about my study of the tabernacle, she said in surprise, "I had no idea God cared about all these details. What difference did it make how big things were or what color they used?" What would your response have been to this comment?

3. What reason would you give for the specific use of bronze in the outer court, silver in the Holy Place, and gold in the Holy of Holies? What would the price of these pounds of metal be on today's market (cost per ounce given daily in the newspaper)?

4. For further study, read about David's plans for the first temple (1 Chronicles 22:5–16; 29:2). See how and why Solomon built the temple (1 Kings 5–6; 2 Chronicles 6:12–13, 7:3). In the back of your study Bible, look for the floor plan of Herod's temple in Jesus' time. What are the similarities in the tabernacle and the two temples?

5. What scripture gives the basis for modern Jewish families to celebrate the Passover and send their children to Hebrew school? Why do you feel Israel has survived against such overwhelming odds?

6.   Why do you feel Aaron and the people turned from God's clear law so quickly and began to worship a golden calf? What golden calves do we have today? What sometimes happens when we put our focus on a person — perhaps our pastor — and lift him up as God on earth?

7.   Do you know anyone so close to God that the person's face glows? What attributes does that person have that set him apart from others?

For Your Notebook

If you are in a group study, make a large floor plan of the tabernacle to use in tracing the steps we will be taking as we enter God's house.

LESSON 15

Dwell in the Desert — And Be Content

Read Exodus 16.

During the construction of the tabernacle, the Israelites continued to live in the desert. There wasn't much choice. When you leave Egypt, there's nowhere to go but desert! Psalm 78:52 states: *He brought his people out like a flock; he led them like sheep through the desert.*

For God's People in Bible Times

At first the children of Israel were so excited over their deliverance at the hand of God that they sang songs of praise, played timbrels, and danced before the Lord. It was "happily-ever-after time," that is, until things got dry in the desert and they yelled to Moses, *"Must we die of thirst?"* (Exodus 15:24, TLB).

If you were God, wouldn't you have gotten tired of those people? Nothing made them happy. They had passed over and passed through. God moved above them in a visible cloud by day and settled in with them as a pillar of fire at night. What more did they want?!

• God gave them water and they cried for food.
• He gave them manna from heaven, fresh each day, and they became greedy.
• He sent quail until they were stuffed with it, and still they complained.

Consulting the Map

God sent His people fresh food each day, and yet they still found reason to complain.

Read Exodus 16:18 and check the box below that best describes how God provided for His people.

◯ He forsook His people, leaving them hungry.

◯ He didn't provide enough food for His people.

◯ He provided food for His people even before they needed it.

◯ He provided exactly enough food for His people when they needed it.

◯ He provided more food than His people needed.

How does Philippians 2:14–15 instruct us to live? Why?

_____

_____

_____

According to Exodus 16:7–8, when we complain, who are we complaining against?

_____

Place an X on the scale below that best describes you.

◯ Never Complain   ◯ Occasionally Complain   ◯ Frequently Complain

Instead of complaining, what does Ephesians 5:20 instruct us to do?

_____

What have you complained about recently?

_____

_____

Instead of complaining, what can you find in the situation to be thankful for?

_____

_____

God's provision is perfect — what you need when you need it. When we complain, we demonstrate a lack of satisfaction with God's sovereignty, and we have no right to complain against God: _Who are you, a mere human being, to criticize God? Should the thing that was created say to the one who made it, "Why have you made me like this?"_ (Romans 9:20, NLT).

Are there some people who are never satisfied? Are there some who want whatever they don't have? Are there those whom even the Lord Himself couldn't please? God had a whole desert full of them — three million murmuring Hebrews crying out for the good ol' days in Egypt. In spite of their fears, God provided for all their needs. Later, Nehemiah reviewed this period when he called out to God:

> "Because of your great compassion you did not abandon them in the desert.... For forty years you sustained them in the desert; they lacked nothing, their clothes did not wear out nor did their feet become swollen."
>
> —Nehemiah 9:19, 21

Consulting the Map

For His people, God provided water, manna, quail, clothes, and shoes that never wore out. All of their needs were provided for.

Look up the following verses and note what you learn about God's provision.

Psalm 23:1

_____

Psalm 84:11

_____

Psalm 145:15–16

_____

Luke 12:28–30

_____

Philippians 4:19

_____

According to Matthew 6:8, when does God know our need?

_____

_____

_____

God promises to provide for *all* of our needs, whether they are physical, emotional, or spiritual. Whether you are financially stressed, consumed by fear and worry, or struggling during a particularly difficult time, God knows your need.

What do you need from Him today?

○ **Grace**   ○ **Peace**   ○ **Freedom from sin**

○ **Healing**   ○ **Financial provision**   ○ **Other:**_____

Rest Stop

Write a prayer to God expressing your need, and then thank Him in advance for His provision: *Do not worry about anything, but pray and ask God for everything you need, always giving thanks* **(Philippians 4:6, NCV)**

_____

_____

_____

_____

_____

For Us in Today's World

How about you? Have you learned to keep your head above water? Are you satisfied with quail and manna — or without either one? Can you say with Paul, *I have learned, in whatsoever state I am, therewith to be content. I know both how to be abased, and I know how to abound: every where and in all things I am instructed both to be full and to be hungry, both to abound and to suffer need* (Philippians 4:11–12, KJV).

Can you also conclude, *I can do all things through Christ which strengtheneth me* (Philippians 4:13, KJV)?

Looking for God takes more than an hour on Sundays. It requires disciplined dedication and the desire to be content in the desert.

Sometimes on our way out of Egypt, God lets us live for a time in the desert. Is that where you are? So many Christians I know were just churchgoers — until they spent some time in the desert of divorce, of poverty, of loneliness, of unforgiveness, of grief, of addictions, of depression, of rejection, of self-pity, of fear, or of disease. But God didn't let them die in the desert! He met their needs, although not always their desires.

Many of us don't take that step of spiritual commitment when our barns are full:

> *When your herds and flocks grow large and your silver and gold increase and all you have is multiplied, then your heart will become proud and you will forget the* LORD *your God, who brought you out of Egypt, out of the land of slavery.*
>
> —Deuteronomy 8:13–14

When God called me out of my Egypt, He sent me to the literal desert of San Bernardino. In retrospect, I see that if He had left me in Connecticut with my big house and prestige in the community, I might have played around on the shores of the Red Sea, dabbling in the good ol' days of Egypt. Instead, He picked up me and my family and moved us from one end of the country to the other, placing us squarely in Bungalow One. While the grounds at Arrowhead Springs might have been a bit like the Garden of Eden, Bungalow One was hardly paradise. Built in the 1930s as a motel, it was shaped much like a train going around a curve. Each of the five rooms had a door opening onto a patio and to go from one room in our bungalow to the other, you had to go outdoors and across the cement. The ceilings were falling in, the rugs were down to the nub, and there was no kitchen. As I cooked on a hot plate on the porch, I cried out, "God, when I sang 'I'll go where You want me to go,' I didn't mean Bungalow One!"

But God did mean Bungalow One, for He knew I needed to spend some time in the desert to shake the Egypt out of me. It was while living in Bungalow One that I started studying the Bible seriously, attending lectures and classes taught by evangelists and theologians, and writing Sunday school lessons. There in the desert, Fred and I created our first marriage class for a local church. This class led to couples seminars and years later became our book, *After Every Wedding Comes a Marriage.* When God wants to get us out of Egypt and into His tabernacle, sometimes He lets us live for a while in the desert.

Surviving a desert experience demands some realistic appraisal of ourselves, for it strips us of pretenses, pulls our props out from under us, and lets us see that we can't do it on our own. We need some outside help that's bigger than we are. Whether your time in the desert is from a broken marriage, a loss of income, or living two years in Bungalow One; whether the cause is physical or emotional, it is usually a humbling, perhaps humiliating, series of events that can make you bitter against life or cause you to reach out for a God who is real.

When Hagar lay crying with her thirsty son in the desert, God knew she had given up just before reaching water. She had quit one step too soon, but *the angel of the LORD found Hagar near a spring in the desert* (Genesis 16:7), and he saved her. God will do no less for you and me. When we cry out in the desert, He will save us.

David, in depression, wanted to *flee far away and stay in the desert* (Psalm 55:7). He could see no way out, but God saved him. As a child, John the Baptist *grew and became strong in spirit; and he lived in the desert until he appeared publicly to Israel* (Luke 1:80). *The word of God came to John...in the desert* (Luke 3:2).

When Paul met the Lord face to face, he had such a startling conversion experience, a total change of drive and motives, that he was eager to become an instant Christian leader. But God sent him to the desert for a time of seasoning, lest he cause more harm than good: *I went immediately into Arabia and later returned to Damascus* (Galatians 1:17).

That's what the Lord did with Fred and me. Excited as we were to evangelize the state of Connecticut, He picked us up from those lush green hills and set us down in a desert far away from our Egypt. He closed the Red Sea behind us. We passed the point of no return, and He said, "Sit here in the desert until you're emptied of self and ready for use." Yes, *He humbles those who dwell on high* (Isaiah 26:5).

Consulting the Map

Abraham, Moses, Paul, and David — great men of the Bible — all spent some time in the desert. It seems that in order for many of us to learn that God is all we need, He first must strip us of all we have.

What did Solomon pray for in Proverbs 30:8–9?

_____

_____

_____

Read 1 Timothy 6:6–7 and then answer the following questions:

How does verse 6 describe contentment?

_____

_____

According to verse 7, why is contentment considered in this way?

_____

_____

What reason does the Lord give us in Hebrews 13:5 to be content?

_____

_____

Are you in a desert right now? How can you apply what you have learned to your situation?

_____

_____

_____

If you are in a desert right now and feel as if you have nothing else in this world, find contentment and satisfaction in knowing Christ. He provided bread from heaven in perfect-sized portions for His people, satisfying their hunger. Likewise, He is your perfect portion, capable of satisfying your soul.

In these days of financial insecurity, many people I know are having to adjust to a different standard of living. This step down can put the family in the desert of depression. But the sooner we accept our situation and put curtains up in Bungalow One, the sooner God will move us on. *Your desert* [will become] *a fertile field* (Isaiah 32:15).

So if you're in the desert today, rejoice; the spring is just ahead! You will become *like streams of water in the desert and the shadow of a great rock in a thirsty land* (Isaiah 32:2).

Don't think for a minute that God has forgotten you. He knows where you are and what lesson He wants you to learn. You may be in the desert, but He's preparing a place for you right now!

Trip Journal

1. When did God first show you that you had to leave Egypt? Under what circumstances? What desires of the past has God changed over the last years? In what other ways do you sense God's direction in your life?

2. In what kind of a desert do you find yourself today? Loneliness? Depression? Self-pity? Can you figure out why God is allowing you to be there? What lesson might He have to teach you before you can become a stream of living water for a thirsty world?

3. Isn't it true of human nature that we cry out for God when we're in need and then forget Him in times of plenty? What is meant by the saying from World War II: "There are no atheists in foxholes"? Why do you feel God decided to come to earth and live in the tabernacle?

Scenic Overlook

When Fred and I were once speaking in Baton Rouge, we met Gary Hendry. He had always been a good person, a member of a wealthy family, an example to the community, a man who did all the right things. He attended a prestigious church and entertained his friends lavishly, expecting nothing in return. He knew who God was, but he'd never spent much time getting to know Him. Suddenly he began to have severe headaches, and tests showed he had a malignant brain tumor. Gary went from the pleasures of Egypt to the desert of disease and despair. With the surgery and excruciating treatments that followed, he lay on his back for months knowing he might not live. In his lucid moments, he began to seek the Lord. He asked for relief from the chemotherapy treatments that caused him to remain in bed. He even promised to spend time encouraging other patients who were in their own peculiar deserts. The doctors wanted him to continue treatment, but because they left him so ill that he was unable to move, he decided that being immobilized was worse than death. He abandoned the prescribed program and did all he could to build up his energy himself. He studied God's Word seriously and soon started visiting cancer patients in hospitals.

"Everyone's looking for God," Gary said. "When they find out their disease is terminal, the first question they ask me has something to do with religion."

He told me of one man who wondered if Gary was a minister. "You must have been sent by God. No one else has come to see me."

Another asked him what church he attended and if they could join while in the hospital.

One patient who had just received the diagnosis of cancer — and who didn't even know who Gary was — begged him to sing old-fashioned hymns, the only touch with God this man could remember. Gary stood beside him and sang while the man cried and clutched his hand. Visitors and nurses paused in the doorway to listen as he led the man to "Just a closer walk with Thee."

Medically speaking, Gary doesn't have a good prognosis, but as long as God sustains him, he'll provide streams of living water in the deserts of disease.

LESSON 16

Seek the Lord — And Enter His Gates

Review Exodus 25–26 and Exodus 33:7–11.
Read Deuteronomy 8:14–19 and Hebrews 8–9.

Just as God prepared a place in the desert for the Hebrews to dwell in His presence, so He also gives us a plan. God wanted to dwell among the children of Israel, but His tabernacle was fenced off and there was only one entrance. Why did He make it so difficult for His people to meet with Him? He wanted each person to care enough to search. Are you willing to follow His map and take another step toward finding God? Let's move out of our tents and seek the Lord where He may be found.

For God's People in Bible Times

Not every Hebrew who had left Egypt and dwelt in the desert cared enough to seek after God and enter His gate. Some were bitter about the circumstances in which they found themselves, some still longed for the good ol' days of Egypt, and some didn't want to worship any God who would build His home in a dry desert far away from civilization. Many began to think of the miracles they had seen as mere coincidences, and they began to be dubious about their traditional God. They had seen the Pharaoh surrounded by possessions in his palace, and they wanted a comparable leader, a God on a throne, a God they could see with their own eyes.

Instead of their dream of the Promised Land, they seemed to be stuck in the desert. Many of them probably thought, *If there really were a God, He surely wouldn't have brought me to a place like this. How could a loving God do this to a good person like me?*

Consulting the Map

God's people were looking at the past through rose-colored lenses. They remembered the good things about Egypt, but they forgot about the bondage that held them there.

Read Isaiah 43:18–19 and answer the following questions.

What does Isaiah instruct us to do in verse 18?

_____

_____

What hope does he give us in verse 19?

_____

What does the Lord promise us in Jeremiah 29:11?

_____

In addition to looking to their past, God's people were so focused on their present situation that they lost sight of the promises God had given them.

Read Hebrews 12:1–2.

What analogy did Paul use in describing the life of a believer (see verse 1)?

_____

Instead of focusing on the things around us, what does Hebrews 12:2 exhort us to do?

_____

According to verse 2, why was Christ willing to "endure the cross"?

_____

Rest Stop

Are you enduring the desert right now? Fix your eyes on Jesus and write a prayer asking God to give you the endurance to finish the race.

Now read Ephesians 3:20. Describe the hope you can find in Him.

_____

_____

The _Life Application Bible_ study notes describe our "desert" experiences this way: "In times of deep trouble, it may appear as though God has forgotten you. But God may be preparing you...for a new beginning with Him at the center."[1]

How often they rebelled against him in the desert and grieved him in the wasteland! (Psalm 78:40). How quickly they forgot His miracles and how often they murmured and complained over their barren desert experience: *They forgot the God who saved them, who had done great things in Egypt, miracles in the land of Ham and awesome deeds by the Red Sea* (Psalm 106:21–22).

Consulting the Map

Even though God's people had witnessed incredible miracles, had been provided for in marvelous ways, and had seen God's very presence in a cloud, they still forgot Him. "To forget" here literally means to willingly neglect — it is not just a temporary lapse of memory.

Read the following scriptures and describe the signs we might see in the life of one who has forgotten God.

Deuteronomy 8:11

_____

Deuteronomy 8:19

_____

Psalm 106:13

_____

Isaiah 51:13

_____

Read Hosea 13:6. What does the Bible indicate is the major factor for forgetting God?

_____

Describe a time in your life when you have neglected God. Which of the above signs were evident in your life?

_____

_____

_____

What drew you back to Him?

_____

_____

When everything in life is going smoothly, we tend to neglect God because we become deluded into thinking that we don't need Him. Remember Him even when everything is going well so you won't be drawn away from Him by the world's pleasures.

So God chose to come to earth and dwell among His people, the same people who were wandering in the wilderness wondering what to do. Once His tabernacle had been completed, God asked His people to seek Him out.

We don't find God by living next door to a church — we have to get up and go to Him. He wants us to _seek the LORD while he may be found; call on him while he is near_ (Isaiah 55:6). He was as near to the Hebrews encamped around His dwelling place as their next-door neighbor, yet _they grumbled in their tents and did not obey the LORD_ (Psalm 106:25).

Imagine how discouraged God must have been with these thankless people who just stayed home and complained. He had chosen to settle into their midst; He had helped them to create a house of God in the desert sands out of materials they had brought with them from Egypt. He had put His very presence in their midst, but they still grumbled in their tents and did not obey the Lord. They wouldn't get up, move toward God, and enter His gate.

For Us in Today's World

How about us? Are we grumbling in our tents, or are we looking for the gate to God? Are we so full of self-pity that we can't go on? Do we say as they must have said: "If there really were a God, why would He leave such a nice person like me alone in the desert?"

Moses said, _"When you are in distress and all these things have happened to you, then in later days you will return to the LORD your God and obey him"_ (Deuteronomy 4:30). He also said that they would find the Lord _"if you look for him with all your heart and with all your soul"_ (Deuteronomy 4:29).

God Himself has said, _"You will seek me and find me when you seek me with all your heart"_ (Jeremiah 29:13).

Consulting the Map

If we want to find the Lord, we must seek Him with all our hearts. If you are feeling like you've been left outside the gate and the Lord seems far away, Scripture tells us what to do.

How does Deuteronomy 4:29 instruct us to seek after God?

_____

According to Job 8:5, how do we seek after God?

_____

What does God promise us in Psalm 91:15?

_____

What three things does Matthew 7:7 command us to do in our search after God?

_____

_____

The *Jamieson-Fausset-Brown Bible Commentary* says, "We *ask* for what we *wish*; we *seek* for what we *miss*; we *knock* for that from which we feel ourselves *shut out*."[2]

In your search for God:
a. What do you wish from God?

_____

b. What do you miss from God?

_____

c. From what are you feeling yourself shut out?

_____

What promise does Matthew 7:8 give us?

_____

_____

_____

God wants us to keep on asking, keep on seeking, and keep on knocking. Unlike the people who had to seek the entrance of the tabernacle to find God, today we're not going to find Him in a certain location, but rather when our search becomes a constant state of mind.

Are you ready to seek for God with all your heart and all your soul? If you are, the Bible has exciting news for you. The Old Testament tabernacle is a symbol of God's presence in us. It is a shadow of things to come; it is a picture of what Jesus would do: *The Word became flesh and made his dwelling among us* (John 1:14).

God takes the "natural elements of creation and transforms them into a symbolic language to depict eternal truths. The tabernacle becomes God's secret code for revealing truth to the sincere and yielding seeker after God.... The tabernacle is God's flannelgraph."[3]

How grateful we should be that we don't have to go to the Sinai Peninsula to find God! We don't even have to build a tent. Instead, the New Testament — the new covenant — allows us to find God in the person of Jesus Christ. Jesus Himself said: *"When I am lifted up from the earth, I will draw everyone to me"* (John 12:32, TEV). *"I and the Father are one"* (John 10:30). *"Understand that the Father is in me"* (verse 38). *"Anyone who has seen me has seen the Father"* (John 14:9).

As a shadow points to the thing that casts it, so the God of the tabernacle foreshadows Christ, our Lord. As Adam was the first man, Christ is the First Man. As Isaac was to be sacrificed by his father, so Jesus — the only begotten Son of God — gave His life for us and became our sacrifice. As Joseph was despised by his brothers, so Christ was also rejected by men. And as Joseph forgave his brothers, so Jesus said, *"Father, forgive them; for they know not what they do"* (Luke 23:34, KJV). As Moses was the savior of his people when he led them from bondage to the Promised Land, so Jesus wants to free us and lead us into eternal life when we believe in Him: *Everyone who calls on the name of the Lord will be saved* (Acts 2:21). *Salvation is found in no one else, for there is no other name under heaven given to men by which we must be saved* (Acts 4:12). In the Old Testament, God came to man in His tabernacle. In the New Testament, and for us, God comes to man in His Son. Jesus is truly the Gate by which we can enter the presence of God.

When I first found that Jesus was the link between the old and new covenants, suddenly the whole Bible came together and made sense. Jesus is the very embodiment of the Old

Testament signs and symbols. The tabernacle wasn't just a tent in the desert, but it was the figure of our everlasting home in heaven: *We know that if the earthly tent we live in is destroyed, we have a building from God, an eternal house in heaven, not built by human hands* (2 Corinthians 5:1).

What a comfort to know, as we have left the bondage of Egypt, dwelt in the desert, and begun seeking the Lord, that He is right here, that this is the right place. He lives among us, and we become temples of His Holy Spirit (1 Corinthians 6:19–20). He has not left us in a dry and thirsty desert, but He's preparing a place for us. And when we are ready to seek Him with all our hearts, He will come and receive us, so that where He is, we may also be (John 14:3).

Don't worry about what you've left behind in Egypt. Instead, *seek ye first the kingdom of God, and his righteousness; and all these things shall be added unto you* (Matthew 6:33, KJV).

For God's People in Bible Times

As the children of Israel sought God in the desert, they soon learned that they couldn't just drop into the tabernacle empty-handed. There was a price to pay to enter into the gates. The Hebrew had to stop his grumbling in the tents, bring a sacrificial lamb, and *enter his gates with thanksgiving and his courts with praise; give thanks to him and praise his name* (Psalm 100:4).

Let's assume that this cheerful Hebrew, carrying his lamb, headed for the house of God to seek forgiveness. He had seen the cloud of God's presence and knew God was there. As he approached, he would see a white linen fence, standing in stark contrast to the black tents in which he and his neighbors lived. The fabric fence was too high to look over and too heavy to look through. He had to find some way to enter into the courts of the Lord.

The fence was a barrier to the man's ability to reach God; to get inside of the tabernacle, he had to be willing to search for the gate with all his heart. When he finally walked around the fence to the east side, he would have found an opening. It wasn't a wrought iron gate or a heavy wooden door; it was a curtain thirty feet wide, woven of blue, purple, scarlet, and white fine-twined linen.

This curtain, custom-designed by God Himself, was not made of coarse fabric as those of us today might use to make an awning, but it was of fine-twined linen, the symbol of righteousness: *Fine linen is the righteousness of saints* (Revelation 19:8, KJV). God specified the colors to be used: blue to represent heaven, God's eternal home; purple to represent royalty; and scarlet to signify the blood atonement and sacrifice for man's sin.

If you remember your grammar-school lessons on color, you recall that both blue and red are primary colors and that when we blend the two, we get purple. Twenty-four times in the book of Exodus these three colors are mentioned in the same order. Since we know God's words are not dropped down by chance, there must be some significance to the sequence; since we know the tabernacle is a foreshadowing of things to come, let's consider how these colors might relate to our Lord Jesus.

Heavenly blue foretells Jesus as the Son of God. The scarlet foretells Jesus as the Son of Man. And the combination of the two, purple, points to the time when the glory of heaven and earth was to be united in one person, our Lord Jesus Christ. Jesus is both God and man. He experienced the pain and feelings of a man with the depth and power of God. His name is *Wonderful Counselor, Mighty God, Everlasting Father, Prince of Peace* (Isaiah 9:6).

The Word was made flesh and dwelt among us!

Supporting the thirty-foot-wide curtain of richly woven fabric were four posts, pillars of acacia wood. The hooks of silver held the folds of linen, and the bases for each post were of bronze. Once inside the gate — the only entrance to the courtyard — the sinner knew he was saved. His acceptance had nothing to do with how important he was in the world or what good works he had done, but only upon his decision to enter the gate into the courtyard with the sacrifice in his arms, his commitment to finding God.

As surely as the Red Sea had shut Egypt out of the Hebrew's life, so the curtain that had kept him outside the courts of God now shut him inside, close to the very presence of God. As David sang, *"A day in thy courts is better than a thousand. I had rather be a doorkeeper in the house of my God, than to dwell in the tents of wickedness"* (Psalm 84:10, KJV).

For Us in Today's World

In our quest for God, we must make the same decision that the Hebrew made: "I want to enter into His gates." In their search for God, many people look in the wrong places. I know one lady who has gone to seminars in every possible mystical field including Zen Buddhism,

T.A. (Transactional Analysis), B'hai, and Confucianism. She told me, "I want to cover all my bases so no matter what they say is the way to heaven, I'll be sure to get there." If only she'd known God's Word! Jesus said, *"I am the door: by me if any man enter in, he shall be saved"* (John 10:9, KJV). And, *"I am the way, the truth, and the life: no man cometh unto the Father, but by me"* (John 14:6, KJV). As there was just one way into the courts of God in Moses' time, there is today one Way, one Door, into the presence of God: *"Verily, verily, I say unto you, He that entereth not by the door...but climbeth up some other way, the same is a thief and a robber"* (John 10:1, KJV).

In his search, the Hebrew would have come up against a wall — and so do we. The white fence around the tabernacle represented the righteousness of God, while their surrounding black tents portrayed the sinfulness of man. For a sinful man to enter into the presence of God, he had to choose to come through the one gate, which, in God's grand design, faced the east, in the light of the rising sun. There's no sneaking in to God via the back way in the dark; He wants us to be out in the open about our commitment to Him.

God has provided for us an open entrance into His presence: Jesus Christ, the Way, the Truth, and the Life. There is no back door to God, but a wide gate in bright light through which we enter His courts with praise.

Many of us stand around the door, knowing that it's there, but not quite wanting to go in. We eye the door as some kind of fire escape; when the flames come, we know where to run. But just knowing where the door is and even occasionally touching the doorpost is not enough. We must make a decision. Do we want to go inside or not? Are we ready to make a commitment to the Lord Jesus? Are we content to remain an outsider?

Let's not wait! Let's make that commitment to our Lord now so that we can enter into His courts with praise. *Commit your way to the LORD; trust in him* (Psalm 37:5).

Rest Stop

Take some time to recommit yourself to entering into God's presence. Pray this simple prayer, or write out your own prayer below.

Dear Jesus, I've been looking for God in some odd places and now I'm standing at Your door. I accept that You are the Way, the Truth, and the Life and that I can't come to God except through You. I make a personal commitment to You and ask that You open the gate that I might come into the very presence of God.

I pray this in the name of Jesus. Amen.

_____

_____

_____

_____

_____

_____

_____

Trip Journal

1. Picture yourself as a parent who loves to spend time with your children, as well as give them gifts. How would you feel if, when they grew older, they wouldn't walk down the street to see you, but just stayed home grumbling and complaining about what you had never given them over the years? Does that thought give you some idea of the discouragement God must have felt when He established His home in the midst of His people and they didn't come rushing to see Him?

2. What similarities do you find between Moses and Jesus in the following areas: In childhood background? In ministry? In miracles? In leadership? In reaction from the people? What does this show you about doing God's work for personal gain or prestige?

Scenic Overlook

Larry was an extremely attractive businessman who conducted seminars on success. He brought me in to speak to one of his groups that met once a month. Before I spoke, he gave the members their "word of the month." He explained that they should write down the word *commitment*, read it every morning, and use it often in conversation. As they focused on this word, they would begin to better understand "commitment."

They all listened to his instructions and dutifully wrote down their "word of the month."

The next morning Larry called me and said he needed to talk with me: Would I go out to lunch with him and his wife? As we sat in a corner booth, Larry looked me right in the eye and asked, "How do you find God?" For a moment, I was stunned; I had never been questioned quite so bluntly!

He continued, "I've always been a good person, but my wife just had a mastectomy, and while she was in the hospital, I was faced with the fact that she might die. I had nowhere to turn; I realized I didn't know God. How do you find Him?"

By then I had regained my composure, and I started with his teaching of the night before. "Remember how you told everyone to concentrate on the word *commitment*? Commitment to what?"

He hesitated and then answered, "Commitment, in general."

"You'll find God when your commitment is specific. A general commitment is an intellectual exercise, but when you commit your life to Jesus, you will come face to face with God."

"I've been committed to good works," he replied, "but somehow when the chips are down, that's not enough."

I explained that good works are commendable but they don't bring you into a personal relationship with the Lord. I shared several verses from Ephesians:

> *For by grace* [God's gift] *are ye saved through faith* [belief, commitment]; *and that not of yourselves* [not from your earnings and strivings]; *it is the gift of God: Not of works* [no matter how impressive yours may have been], *lest any man should boast* [or take the credit].
> —Ephesians 2:8–9, KJV

"But I'm a self-made man who's committed to excellence," Larry replied.

"There's nothing wrong with good motives," I said, "but you won't find the peace of God until your commitment is to Jesus. You have to give up your own will and present yourself as a living sacrifice to the Lord."

I had to assure Larry that a commitment to Jesus was not a "weak" thing to do, but that it took a strong man to recognize he needed a power beyond himself. I explained that Paul, a man's man, was not ashamed of being a Christian. He wrote, *"I know whom I have believed, and am persuaded that he is able to keep that which I have committed unto him against that day"* (2 Timothy 1:12, KJV).

"He'll only keep that which you have committed, Larry. Can you sacrifice your will and commit your life to Jesus?"

Larry was looking for success in life in a word. That day he found meaning to life in *the* Word!

LESSON 17

Pay the Price — And Be Set Free

Read Leviticus 1–7, 17.

We've all heard the expression, "There's no such thing as a free lunch. Somebody has to pay." When we go to a concert or fly on a plane, we need a ticket. We have to pay the price. So it was for the Hebrews who wanted to enter the gate and come near to God. Even though they were out in the desert, they still had their own currency and a system for using it.

During the forty years the Israelites wandered in the wilderness, the "shekel of the sanctuary" was their medium of exchange and was always looked upon as a divinely ordained coin. Each Hebrew personally paid half a shekel of silver to the Lord on his twentieth birthday. In other offerings, each person gave according to his ability, but in the matter of atonement — making each person "at one" with God — everyone was at the same level. The amount of silver was set low enough so that everyone could pay, showing that God didn't accept a person according to his wealth. By paying his atonement money, the Hebrew was declared "not guilty."

Consulting the Map

According to Acts 8:23, what holds us in bondage?

_____

What does Romans 3:23 say about humankind in general?

_____

We tend to think of sin in varying degrees. What insight regarding "degrees of sin" do you gain by reading Galatians 5:19–21?

_____

_____

Because of the state of our souls, a ransom is required. Read Matthew 20:28. Who paid our ransom and what did it cost?

_____

For God's People in Bible Times

Not only did the Hebrew of old have to pay his atonement half-shekel, he also had to bring an offering to his God. Since the ritual of the tabernacle was new and they had never made a sin offering before, Moses had to educate the people and teach them how to approach God with a gift in hand. As the Hebrew entered the courtyard and brought his sacrifice, the first thing he saw was the altar — the focal point and the centerpiece, literally "the killing place."[1] He could not step around it; he had to go straight to it. There was no access to God without first making a sacrifice. Sin could only be forgiven by the substitution of an animal for the sinner himself — an innocent animal had to die in place of the guilty man.

Consulting the Map

Unlike the Hebrews, we are no longer required to present a sacrifice before approaching God, although a sacrifice is still required. According to Hebrews 9:22, what does the law require? According to John 19:34, how has Jesus fulfilled the law?

Read each of the following verses and record what you learn about the sacrifice Christ made for you.

Acts 20:28

_____

_____

Galatians 4:4–5

_____

_____

Ephesians 1:7

_____

_____

1 Timothy 2:5–6

_____

_____

Titus 2:14

_____

_____

Hebrews 9:12

_____

_____

1 Peter 1:18–19

_____

_____

Christ came to earth and paid the price for a debt He didn't owe, so that you could have access to God. The Easton's Illustrated Dictionary says it this way: "The debt against us is not viewed as simply cancelled, but is fully paid. Christ's blood or life ... is the 'ransom' by which the deliverance of his people from the servitude of sin and from its penal consequences is secured."[2]

The altar of acacia wood overlaid with bronze was a square that was seven-and-a-half feet wide and three feet high (Exodus 27:1, TLB). This was no "holy hibachi," but a huge bronze altar with a horn on each corner used to bind the victim over the fire: _Bind the sacrifice with cords, even unto the horns of the altar"_ (Psalm 118:27, KJV). The four horns represented the four sides of the fence where the tribes were in tents, and ultimately the four corners of the world. It indicated that all people everywhere would eventually have access to God's forgiveness. This altar was a place where God's authority passed judgment on the sinner and his substitutionary lamb.

The fire in the altar was never allowed to go out, showing God's constancy and availability at all times to forgive sin. But before the Hebrew could take one step further toward God, he had to satisfy the demands of the altar. The blood sacrifice is where a walk with God begins.

There were five types of offerings that could be brought to the tabernacle: the trespass offering, the sin offering, the burnt offering, the meal offering, and the peace offering.

The *trespass offering*:

Jesus taught us to pray, "Forgive us our trespasses as we forgive those who trespass against us." A *trespass* is a sin that is knowingly committed. This particular offering was to make atonement for such sins and to remove the guilt from sins of the past. It was not so much the person as the evil deed itself that was the focus of this offering. As one draws nearer to God, he begins to realize, perhaps for the first time, that things he did in the past were sins in the sight of God.

The *sin offering*:

This offering was to make restitution for sins committed in innocence or ignorance, those unknown things that produce a guilty conscience and need to be purged: *If a person sins and does what is forbidden in any of the LORD's commands, even though he does not know it, he is guilty and will be held responsible* (Leviticus 5:17). Ignorance of the law is no excuse.

From his own flock, the Hebrew brought his sacrificial animal, without blemish or spot. He was to bring God the best that he had to offer, not some poor sick lamb that was about to die anyway. As he brought the animal to the altar, it would *be accepted for him to make atonement for him* (Leviticus 1:4, KJV). *Atonement* meant a "covering over;" the blood of the animal stood for and covered over the guilty man who laid his hand on the animal's head, identifying with it and becoming "at one" with it. He then killed it himself.

Two substitutions took place: The animal was a substitution for the sinner; then the priest took over and substituted for the sinner by completing the ritual. When the blood was poured out upon the base of the altar, the sinner was forgiven and free, cleansed by the blood of the lamb. *Blessed is he whose transgressions are forgiven, whose sins are covered. Blessed is the man whose sin the LORD does not count against him* (Psalm 32:1–2).

The other three offerings were the "sweet savor" offerings, to be given in thanksgiving.

The *burnt offering*:

The burnt offering or ascending offering was presented to God for His pleasure and delight, resulting in a feeling of acceptance for the one presenting it: *The LORD taketh pleasure in his people* (Psalm 149:4, KJV). The intent of the offering was not to beg for forgiveness, but to ask for acceptance; it was not based on the individual's merit, but upon God's mercy.

The *meal offering*:

This offering was to be food for the priest made of fine flour that had not been sifted or bruised, representing God's perfection and holiness. Oil — the symbol for the Holy Spirit — was poured over it, and frankincense, indicating purity and fragrance, was added. The hotter the fire got, the more beautiful the aroma became. No leaven (which represented sin) and no honey (which represented human sweetness easily turned sour under fire) was to be used. Salt was added for flavor and as a preservative.

The *peace offering*:

This offering was shared by Jehovah, the priest, and the individual, and it was a prototype of our communion table. The offering satisfied God, and the priest came to peace with the one who brought it and was free to share, minister, and break bread with the forgiven sinner.

For Us in Today's World

Just as man in the Old Testament could approach God only at the altar, we, too, can come close to God in only one way — through His Son, Jesus Christ: *"He that hath seen me hath seen the Father"* (John 14:9, KJV). Although many churches and evangelists put emphasis on the need to give money, God doesn't require even half a shekel from us for us to be acceptable to Him. Our salvation is a free gift, costing nothing: *For by grace are ye saved through faith; and that not of yourselves: it is the gift of God: Not of works, lest any man should boast* (Ephesians 2:8–9, KJV). If we could buy our way to heaven or openly work to achieve greatness, then only those with wealth or talent would be acceptable and able to find God. But as in the Old Testament, the door is open to each one of us to come face to face with God. For us the door is Jesus, and He has already laid Himself on the altar for us: *Ye were not redeemed with corruptible things, as silver and gold,... but with the precious blood of Christ* (1 Peter 1:18–19, KJV).

When we present ourselves at the ticket booth, we find our way has already been paid. We don't have to put up even a half-shekel, but we do have to offer up a sacrifice of our own free will. Does that mean we must bring a lamb without spot or blemish to church with us every week? How do we lay our gift on the altar?

We must first realize that the actual shedding of the animal's blood did not physically change the life of the sinner. It was an outward sign that he was willing to confess to God and give Him an offering to represent his inner nature so that his guilt might be relieved. Every time he sinned he was to present himself to God for absolution, but there would never be a time when he would pay the price completely.

For us, God sent His perfect Son, the Lamb of God who takes away the sins of the world. He becomes our substitute as the lamb became the substitute for the Hebrews. No longer do we have to trudge to the altar with a lamb; Christ has paid it all.

I had heard all these terms as a child. But until I understood the pattern God gave at the tabernacle, I had no idea why Christ was called a lamb, why He had "paid it all," why we were cleansed by the blood. Things that sounded demeaning, almost offensive, suddenly made sense. The tabernacle was a foretelling of what Christ was going to do for you and me. Now I could understand why John said, *"Behold the Lamb of God, which taketh away the sin of the world"* (John 1:29, KJV). Now I knew why Peter explained that we are redeemed by *the precious blood of Christ, as of a lamb without blemish and without spot* (1 Peter 1:19, KJV), why Paul wrote, *God made Him who had no sin to be sin for us, so that in him we might become the righteousness of God* (2 Corinthians 5:21).

The *trespass offering* for us:

One of the first things a new believer experiences as he seeks fellowship with God is an overwhelming awareness of sin in his life. White lies (previously explainable acts), rebellious attitudes, loose morals, swearing, critical words, and other patterns of behavior that had appeared "above average" when out in the world, suddenly are seen as sin.

But our Father in heaven forgives our trespasses: *You were dead in sins, and your sinful desires were not yet cut away. Then he gave you a share in the very life of Christ, for he forgave all your sins* (Colossians 2:13, TLB).

The *sin offering* for us:

As we become aware of our sins and confess these trespasses to the Lord, He forgives us of these specific acts. But our second awareness comes when we realize that our *whole nature* is self-centered and that we continue to sin despite our good intentions. We find that we must continue to bring our sin offering to the Lord and confess our rebellious attitudes as well as our deeds. As the Hebrew people did, we, too, must bring a sacrifice for our sins of ignorance. We are not to sit in ignorance forever, using that as an excuse to test God's grace, but we are to study His Word in an effort to become aware of any ways in which we might be displeasing to Him.

We are to, as Paul says, put off the old man with his deeds, our old nature, and put on the new man *renewed in knowledge after the image of him that created him* (Colossians 3:10, KJV). To change requires a step of action. We are not to just sit there in our sins, saying, "If God wants me to be different, He knows where to find me."

The sin offering was to be without blemish — and that eliminates us and any animal we might find. But we can rejoice, for Jesus is our Lamb without blemish or spot. We will never be good enough to get to heaven on our own merit, but we don't have to.

> *God has shown us a different way to heaven — not by "being good enough" and trying to keep his laws, but by a new way.... Now God says he will accept and acquit us — declare us "not guilty" — if we trust Jesus Christ to take away our sins. And we all can be saved in this same way, by coming to Christ, no matter who we are or what we have been like. Yes, all have sinned; all fall short of God's glorious ideal; yet now God declares us "not guilty" of offending him if we trust in Jesus Christ, who in his kindness freely takes away our sins.*
>
> —Romans 3:21–24, TLB

Yes, Jesus has paid it all, but God still wants a personal sacrifice from each one of us, and it doesn't involve building an altar in the backyard and killing a spotless lamb. David, who understood and practiced the Old Testament ceremonies of sacrifice, finally caught the spirit of the ritual after his sin of adultery with Bathsheba. When he realized he had violated one of the commandments he himself had taught to others, he cried out in repentance to God: *"You do not delight in sacrifice, or I would bring it; you do not take pleasure in burnt offerings. The sacrifices of God are a broken spirit; a broken and contrite heart, O God, you will not despise"* (Psalm 51:16–17).

David was saying, "I know the rules, and I have money. I could give You the best bull and the whitest lamb You've ever seen and say, 'Here it is, Lord. Forgive me.' I could try to buy my way to salvation, but that's not what You want of me. You want a repentant heart, a broken spirit. You want me to accept the blame for my sin and give You a genuinely contrite heart, not animals. Wash me with Your blood and make me, a sinner, white as snow" (see Psalm 51).

Paul "beseeches" us, begs us, pleads with us — knowing that it won't be easy for many — to present our *bodies a living sacrifice, holy, acceptable unto God, which is* [our] *reasonable service* (Romans 12:1, KJV). Paul is asking us to lay ourselves on the altar as Abraham laid Isaac, as the Hebrew laid the lamb, and as Jesus laid Himself. We are to present our bodies as a living sacrifice — in contrast to the death of the lamb. God does not want you and me to sign some death pact and commit suicide as our sacrifice. He wants us to stay very much alive, but to give up our strong wills; He wants us to give control of our lives over to Him. This "giving up" of self is a holy act, much like that in which the Old Testament Hebrew gave up his offering. When we understand that He wants us, not an animal, doesn't that become a "reasonable service"?

Consulting the Map

Since Christ was willing to die for our sins, we should be willing to sacrifice our will and live for Him.

Read 1 Corinthians 6:19–20 and explain why He deserves our sacrifice.

_____

_____

How does 1 Peter 1:13–19 describe how those redeemed by Christ should live?

_____

_____

Look up the following verses and note how the Bible instructs us to live a holy life.

Matthew 5:48

_____

2 Corinthians 7:1

_____

Ephesians 5:1–2

_____

Philippians 1:27–28

_____

Philippians 2:15–16

_____

1 Thessalonians 4:3–7

_____

Titus 2:11–13

_____

Titus 3:8

_____

Hebrews 12:14–15

_____

2 Peter 1:4–9

_____

With these scripture passages in mind, in which areas of your life are you lacking holiness?

_____

_____

_____

Sometimes living a holy life requires sacrifice. What sacrifices do you need to make in order to live a holy life before God?

_____

_____

_____

Choosing to be holy is seldom easy. Jesus responded to the rich young ruler by saying, *"Take up the cross, and follow me"* (Mark 10:21, KJV). If we are not willing to take up our cross to follow Him, we are not worthy of Him.

God asks us to *be not conformed to this world,* but to be *transformed* (Romans 12:2, KJV). He wants to renew our minds, erase the guilt, and sharpen up our thinking so that we can begin to get a glimpse of His good, acceptable, and perfect will for each one of us.

How gracious of God to send His Son as Savior, substitute, and example of how we should present ourselves — body, mind, and spirit — as living sacrifices. Jesus has paid the price that we might have the free gift of eternal life.

Oswald Chambers sums it up so well:

> God pays no respect to anything we bring Him: there is only one thing God wants of us and that's our unconditional surrender.... The natural life is not spiritual and it can only be made spiritual by sacrifice. If we do not resolutely sacrifice the natural, the supernatural can never become natural in us. Beware of refusing to go to the funeral of your own independence.[3]

The *burnt offering* for us:

This offering had little to do with sin but was praise given to God for His pleasure. It was presented as if to say: "I know I'm not a perfect person, but I love You and I want to be accepted as Your child, identified with You. I'm presenting myself as a living sacrifice, hoping to be holy and wanting to be acceptable in Your sight."

How exciting it is to finally come to the realization that Christ stood in for me! I can never be good enough on my own, but when I am totally identified with Christ, I have become worthy and acceptable. I can't stand before a holy God on my own, but only as Jesus increases in my life and my spirit becomes more like His. I am no longer a lost sinner looking for God, but I am in His presence and He approves of me! Christ gave *himself for us an offering and a sacrifice to God for a sweetsmelling savour* (Ephesians 5:2, KJV). He stood in for you and me, and God the Father is pleased!

The *meal offering* for us:

This food, presented to the priest, was a representation of the Lord Jesus, the perfect man, who said of Himself:

> *"I am the true Bread from heaven; and anyone who eats this Bread shall live forever, and not die as your fathers did — though they ate bread from heaven."*
> —John 6:58, TLB

Jesus is our meal offering made of fine flour. *God anointed Jesus of Nazareth with the Holy Ghost and with power* (Acts 10:38, KJV). He had the oil of the Spirit, the purity and aroma of frankincense. There was no leaven, no sin, in Him, nor was there any need for the added sweetness of honey. His message was not bland or without salt, but clear and pungent. He was the salt of the earth that had not lost its savor.

Although you and I can't physically lay the Lord on the altar as a meal offering, we can serve, feed, and minister to others in His name, knowing that he who offers a cup of cool water to anyone in Jesus' name has given it to Jesus Himself.

The *peace offering* for us:

As the burnt offering was only for Jehovah God, the peace offering was meant to be shared with others. God received His portion (the fat parts of a bullock, a lamb, or a goat, which were burnt on the altar), and then the priest received his portion (the breast that was waved and the thigh that was presented), to be eaten by his family in a holy place (see Leviticus 7:30–34). This offering was a forerunner of the communion table that Christ shared with His disciples, and it is an example for us today as we partake of the bread and the wine.

Paul wrote, *Is not the cup of thanksgiving for which we give thanks a participation in the blood of Christ? And is not the bread that we break a participation in the body of Christ?* (1 Corinthians 10:16).

And,

> *Whoever eats the bread or drinks the cup of the Lord in an unworthy manner will be guilty of sinning against the body and blood of the Lord. A man ought to examine himself before he eats of the bread and drinks of the cup. For anyone who*

eats and drinks without recognizing the body of the Lord eats and drinks judgment on himself.

—1 Corinthians 11:27–29

As the blood of the lamb cleansed the Hebrew of his sins, the blood of the Lamb, sacrificed for you and for me, cleanses us. Jesus Himself said, as He gave His disciples a symbolic cup, *"This is my blood of the new testament, which is shed for many for the remission of sins"* (Matthew 26:28, KJV).

How important it is for us to understand the Old Testament so that we can fully grasp the meaning of the New! How exciting communion could become for us if we would catch the deep concept of why Jesus died *for the remission of sins,* and could see that Jesus paid the price once and for all.

He did not enter by means of the blood of goats and calves; but he entered the Most Holy Place once for all by his own blood, having obtained eternal redemption.... Without the shedding of blood there is no forgiveness.

—Hebrews 9:12, 22

As we continue our journey to Jesus, to a closer walk with Him, we have to leave our worldly conformity in Egypt, keep our faith in the heat of our own personal desert, and seek the Lord with all our hearts, leaning not to our own understanding. There is only one Way. Christ has paid the price and we are free!

Trip Journal

1. Now that you have a better understanding of the floor plan of the tabernacle, what interpretation do you have of Psalm 100:4: *Enter into his gates with thanksgiving, and into his courts with praise* (KJV)? And, Psalm 84:10: *For a day in thy courts is better than a thousand. I had rather be a doorkeeper in the house of my God, than to dwell in the tents of wickedness* (KJV)? How does this view differ from what you might have thought in the past?

2. What fence did, or does, stand between you and a relationship with God? Why do you think there was no "back door" into the courtyard? What significance is there to you in the verse that says, *"I am the door"*? (See John 10:7, KJV.)

3. What is the difference in the cost of the Hebrew coming to God and the price we pay to come to God?

4. How do the trespass offering and sin offering differ? How may you have seen this difference in your own life?

5. What have you done recently just for the joy of pleasing God? When have you last presented a "meal offering" for your pastor or another Christian worker?

For Your Notebook

Do a study on the word *blood,* using a concordance and a Bible dictionary. A deeper understanding of the importance God puts on this fluid is so necessary for life and forgiveness.

> *For the life of the flesh is in the blood: and I have given it to you upon the altar to make an atonement for your souls: for it is the blood that maketh an atonement for the soul.*
> —Leviticus 17:11, KJV

LESSON 18

Follow the Leader — And Be Cleansed

Review Exodus 28–29; then read Leviticus 1–9.

When God designed the tabernacle and its furnishings, He could have left it unattended, expecting each person to find their own way from the gate into the presence of God. But because He wanted the people to have access to Himself, He appointed priests and ordained them to carry out the sacrifices and other duties exactly as He prescribed. In that way, all those who were seeking would find the Lord.

For God's People in Bible Times

God did not have personnel records or standard job descriptions to work with — so how did He make His choice for these important leadership positions? If you were God, where would you find such qualified men out in a desert? There were twelve tribes to choose from, and not one of them was noted for its godliness.

For a résumé on each of Jacob's sons, let's look at Genesis 49, which records the comments given by Jacob when he called his sons together at his deathbed. The following list is a summary of what he had to say about each of his sons. As you read, think about which one you would choose as a high priest.

Reuben:
You are the oldest but the most unruly. You slept with one of my wives, dishonored me, and were not repentant. Because of that, I'm demoting you, and you will not receive the double portion of the firstborn.

Simeon and Levi:
You are two of a kind, men of violence and injustice, murderers, angry, fierce, and cruel. I will scatter your descendants throughout Israel.

Judah:

Your brothers shall praise you. You are like a powerful lion and from you will come kings.

Zebulun:

You shall live by the sea, with your borders extending through the land.

Issachar:

You are a strong beast of burden and will work hard on the land.

Dan:

You are like a serpent in the path that bites the horses' heels and causes the riders to fall off.

Gad:

You will be pursued, but you will defend your land.

Asher:

You will produce rich foods fit for kings.

Naphtali:

You are like a deer let loose, producing lovely fawns.

Joseph:

You were severely injured by your own brothers who sold you as a slave. Because you remained steady, you will become as a fruitful tree beside a fountain with branches shading the wall. May God's blessings on you reach to the utmost bounds of the everlasting hills and may your sons be blessed as you receive a double portion through Ephraim and Manasseh.

Benjamin:

You are like a wolf on the prowl who devours his enemies each morning.

Consulting the Map

While the résumés from which God had to choose did not sound too promising, they were an accurate report from Jacob who had observed the lives of his sons. What do people see when they observe your life?

Read the following verses and note the traits that should be visible in a person who loves God. Put a checkmark next to the ones you think people would say about you. If you are really brave, you might ask your family and friends for their input here.

○ **Jeremiah 24:7** ○ **Micah 6:8** ○ **Romans 14:17**

○ **2 Corinthians 6:6–7** ○ **Ephesians 5:3** ○ **Philippians 4:8**

○ **Colossians 3:12–15** ○ **1 Timothy 6:11** ○ **Titus 2:7–8**

○ **1 Peter 4:8** ○ **2 Peter 1:5–7**

Using your Bible concordance, find at least one other passage of Scripture that addresses the evidence of the Lord in our lives. (Hint: They are sometimes referred to as the "fruit" of the Christian life.) Write out that passage here:

_____

_____

_____

_____

_____

Rest Stop

If there are any of the above points of a Christian résumé that are not evident in your life, stop now and pray to God for His power to help you manifest the missing qualities. Write your prayer below.

_____

_____

_____

_____

_____

_____

_____

If you were in God's position, which tribe would you choose to be the family of priests and to serve you in your new home on earth? If I were making a "spiritual" selection, I might cancel out Reuben, Simeon, Levi, Dan, and Benjamin for their bad records in the past. Zebulun and Gad sound inoffensive but dull. Issachar was a hard worker, certainly a commendable trait for a man of ministry, and Asher and his descendants were good cooks. Perhaps those two tribes could take care of all my needs. Naphtali would make me nervous by leaping around like a deer. Judah is the logical choice as his descendants were to produce kings, but sometimes so-called important people don't have a servant's heart. In the final analysis, the tribes stemming from Joseph seem to deserve the position. When I consider the humiliation Joseph suffered at the hands of these brothers, I could make no other choice!

God made an unlikely selection, however. He put the call and the anointing upon the tribe of Levi, a cruel and angry man. Does God make mistakes — or does He sometimes choose a person unqualified in the eyes of the world in order to show His transforming power? Even today, many of God's most noted servants come out of backgrounds that would seem to disqualify them for Christian leadership. How God loves to take the foolish things of the world to confound the wise. When Saul was chosen by Samuel to be the first king of the Israelites, his friends were dumbfounded over the selection. They asked each other, *"What is this that has happened to the son of Kish? Is* [the Old Testament's] *Saul also among the prophets?... How can this fellow save us?"* (1 Samuel 10:11, 27). Only God could have seen any commendable qualities in the New Testament's Saul of Tarsus as he murdered Christians. And only God would have taken a chance on transforming him into Paul, the great evangelist who could convince others of the power of God to change lives.

Yes, God is all-powerful, and He delights in taking any unlikely person and transforming them before the eyes of a skeptical world. So God chose Aaron to be the first high priest and his fellow Levites to serve with him. This Aaron was the same Aaron who served as a mouthpiece for his brother, Moses, in Egypt, the same one who invited the complaining Hebrews to an orgy while Moses was on the mountain communing with God, the same immature person who made a golden calf out of the women's jewelry and then blamed it all on them — "You know these people. They are bent on mischief! Surely it wasn't my fault."

No wonder God told Moses to take Aaron aside and wash him with water before the dedication. Moses washed him completely, cleansing him of his old life. God's power caused Aaron to be transformed into a new creature, the high priest of Israel.

Consulting the Map

Aaron is just one example in Scripture of a man whom, without the most glowing résumé, God still decided to use. Perhaps you have felt that God could not use you because of your past behavior.

Read the following verses and note what God says about a life that is transformed. Can a life be changed?

Romans 7:4

_____

_____

2 Corinthians 3:18

_____

_____

Ephesians 4:20–24

_____

_____

Colossians 3:10

_____

_____

Based on the above verses, what is the key to change?

_____

_____

From then on, the one-time cleansing of the old life and the daily washing away of new sinful deeds before serving God became a ritual for the priests. To facilitate the frequent cleansing process, God said to Moses:

> _Make a bronze basin with a bronze pedestal. Put it between the Tabernacle and_
> _the altar, and fill it with water. Aaron and his sons shall wash their hands and feet_

there, when they go into the Tabernacle to appear before the LORD, *or when they approach the altar to burn offerings to the* LORD. *They must always wash before doing so, or they will die.*

—Exodus 30:17–20, TLB

The bronze washbasin and its bronze pedestal were cast from the solid bronze mirrors donated by the women who assembled at the entrance to the Tabernacle.

—Exodus 38:8, TLB

Isn't it fascinating that God used the mirror, a symbol of self-examination, to make a basin for the purpose of washing the sin of "self" away?

For Us in Today's World

Paul wrote: *We can be mirrors that brightly reflect the glory of the Lord. And as the Spirit of the Lord works within us, we become more and more like Him* (2 Corinthians 3:18, TLB). And, *God is always at work in you to make you willing and able to obey his own purpose* (Philippians 2:13, TEV).

As God assigned Moses to wash the priests before they were to serve Him, so Jesus wants to cleanse you and me of sin in our lives. He wants us to come before Him and agree with Him that we need to be changed: *If we confess our sins, he is faithful and just to forgive us our sins, and to cleanse us from all unrighteousness* (1 John 1:9, KJV).

When we present ourselves as an offering before Christ, our High Priest, He forgives us; as we recognize and confess our sin, He cleanses us. We are saved by the blood of Jesus *once* and cleansed by the water of forgiveness and restoration *daily*. Salvation is a one-time act of faith, but as we make mistakes and don't live according to God's will, we need to seek His forgiveness and cleansing each day.

As Paul wrote to Titus:

Not by works of righteousness which we have done, but according to his mercy he saved us, by the washing of regeneration, and renewing of the Holy Ghost.

—Titus 3:5, KJV

We can be born again and given a new, clean life, no matter what our past behavior may have been. So:

> *Let us draw near with a true heart in full assurance of faith, having our hearts*
> *sprinkled from an evil conscience, and our bodies washed with pure water.*
> —Hebrews 10:22, KJV

Let us praise Christ as our High Priest: *Him that loved us, and washed us from our sins in his own blood* (Revelation 1:5, KJV). Frequently I talk with people who feel God couldn't possibly accept them. Some are innocent victims of childhood abuse who still feel they were to blame. Some have done terrible things they assume God could never forgive. Some have habits that the local church they want to join will not accept.

A God who would choose to transform the Levites into spiritual leaders, and a man like Aaron into a high priest, Saul into a king, or Paul into an evangelist can surely "clean up" any one of us if we'll only ask.

> *Having therefore these promises, dearly beloved, let us cleanse ourselves from all*
> *filthiness of the flesh and spirit, perfecting holiness in the fear of God.*
> —2 Corinthians 7:1, KJV

For God's People in Bible Times

As we have seen, priests were not chosen because of their training, education, wealth, character, spirituality, or personal holiness. God chose ordinary people, set them apart, and sanctified them for His service. So often today, as I train people to be Christian leaders, they will say, "God could never use me;" then they provide a laundry list of their flaws, not understanding that God doesn't need credentials. He confers His own degrees.

When God chose Aaron to represent Him, He proclaimed:

> *"Make special clothes for Aaron, to indicate his separation to God — beautiful*
> *garments that will lend dignity to his work. Instruct those to whom I have given*
> *special skill as tailors to make the garments that will set him apart from others,*
> *so that he may minister to me in the priest's office."*
> —Exodus 28:2–3, TLB

How beautiful were Aaron's clothes to be? The first garment placed on Aaron was a white linen coat, representing the purity and holiness of God. Next came *the curious girdle* (Exodus 28:8, KJV), or belt, tying his undercoat to his body and signifying his willingness to serve. Over this was placed a robe of blue, the color of heaven, showing that he had been chosen by God, not by man.

For those of you who thought the "layered look" was a new idea, picture an ephod draped over the white coat, girdle, and blue robe. The ephod was a special item worn only by the high priest — the best way for us to imagine it today is as a type of cobbler's apron: two pieces of cloth joined at the shoulders. As was the curtain at the gate of the tabernacle, the ephod was woven of fine-twined linen of blue, purple, and scarlet. Added to this were fine wires of gold interlaced into the material — done with *cunning work* (Exodus 28:6, KJV).

If these were not enough, there were added two stones of onyx to be worn on the shoulders of the high priest. Each of these stones was to be engraved with the names of one of the twelve tribes: six on each shoulder in the order of their birth. These two large stones, estimated to be ninety-five carats apiece, were set in gold and joined to the ephod by gold rope chains. As the high priest moved about, these stones faced up to heaven, constantly carrying the names of the twelve tribes before the Lord as a reminder.

Hung on the front of the priest was a breastplate — not a heavy metal shield, as it might sound to us, but a nine-by-eighteen-inch piece of linen fabric of blue, purple, and scarlet interlaced with gold. This cloth was folded in half, making a nine-by-nine-inch square with a pocket in the bottom to carry the *Urim* and *Thummim,* the divining stones used to determine the Lord's will. Attached to the front of this linen square were four rows of three stones apiece, each stone representing a tribe.

Can you imagine the beauty and brilliance of this array of gemstones? Picture the largest cut stone you've ever seen and multiply it by twelve. This will give you some idea of how spectacular the breastplate was and of how God wanted His priest to stand out in the crowd.

This jewel-encrusted cloth was attached to the ephod by gold ropes threaded through gold rings. At the bottom, the blue fabric, representing heaven, was tied down with the blue ribbons of obedience. These same blue ribbons were placed on the borders of garments for generations as an earthly sign of obedience to a heavenly God.

Put upon the fringe of the borders a ribband of blue; And it shall be unto you for a fringe, that ye may look upon it, and remember all the commandments of the LORD, and do them.

—Numbers 15:38–39, KJV

Again, God was specific when He instructed that the neck opening of the ephod be bound in gold so that it would not fray, and the bottom edge be lined with gold bells that would tinkle when Aaron came into the presence of God. This breastplate was what we might call a large prayer list, keeping the needs of the people before God.

In this way Aaron shall carry the names of the tribes of Israel on the chestpiece over his heart (it is God's oracle) when he goes in to the Holy Place; thus Jehovah will be reminded of them continually.

—Exodus 28:29, TLB

On his head, the high priest was to wear a turban made of white linen. His head was to be covered, as a sign to God that he was submissive and obedient. This diadem, mitre, or crown was also an indication of royal status, thus combining the idea of kingship and humility. Across the front of the turban, tied on with blue ribbons, was a plate of pure gold engraved with the words: *Consecrated to Jehovah.*

In this way Aaron will be wearing it upon his forehead, and thus bear the guilt connected with any errors regarding the offerings of the people of Israel. It shall always be worn when he goes into the presence of the LORD, so that the people will be accepted and forgiven.

—Exodus 28:37–38, TLB

After Aaron was properly clothed, he and his brothers were officially consecrated to the Lord. Aaron put on his white coat, curious girdle, blue robe, ornately woven ephod, bejeweled breastplate, white turban, and engraved gold medallion. These seven items were worn during the seven days of dedication.

Consulting the Map

Aaron and the Levites had to prepare themselves before they entered the presence of God.

Read the following verses that address the issue of preparing to meet God in worship. Based on God's Word, what are your thoughts about how you prepare to meet God?

Genesis 35:2

_____

_____

_____

Exodus 19:10–14

_____

_____

_____

Numbers 8:7

_____

_____

_____

2 Samuel 12:20

_____

_____

_____

1 Peter 3:3–4

_____

_____

_____

Moses, under instruction from God, commissioned the anointing oil to be made by skilled perfume makers. The mixture contained eighteen pounds each of pure myrrh and cassia, nine pounds of cinnamon and sweet cane, and one and one-half gallons of pure olive oil (see Exodus 30:22–24, TLB). This special oil was to be used for holy dedication only. God said:

"It must never be poured upon an ordinary person, and you shall never make any of it yourselves, for it is holy, and it shall be treated by you as holy. Anyone who compounds any incense like it or puts any of it upon someone who is not a priest shall be excommunicated."

—Exodus 30:32–33, TLB

A special offering of the ram of consecration was also made at the dedication of Aaron and his sons as priests. Moses put the blood of the ram on the Levites' right ears, right thumbs, and right foot's big toes. After their dedication, the priests were to serve as intercessors, connectors, and go-betweens. As the guilty sinner came to them at the altar with his sacrifice, the priests were to stand in for him, and the high priest with his breastplate of names was to continually bring them all before the Lord. The high priest became the connecting link between sinful man and a holy God. He represented the people much as a lawyer would stand in for a client; he was the line of communication between the caller and the receiver (see Exodus 29).

For Us in Today's World

How do you and I find God when we don't have Aaron around and our names aren't permanently engraved on precious gemstones? Who is our intercessor? Do we need some holy man in a strange-looking costume to hold us before God? Who is to be our leader?

The book of Hebrews tells us the answer: *Jesus was faithful to God who appointed him High Priest, just as Moses also faithfully served in God's house* (Hebrews 3:2, TLB).

Christ ... is our High Priest, and is in heaven at the place of greatest honor next to God himself. He ministers in the temple in heaven, the true place of worship built by the Lord and not by human hands.

—Hebrews 8:1–2, TLB

Our Jesus wears the white robe of righteousness and the girdle of a servant. As the high priest, who served in the tabernacle and bore the names of the twelve tribes on his shoulders, so our High Priest carries each one of us before the throne of our Father in heaven.

As Aaron carried the separate tribes before God on his bosom, so our Lord *poured out his life unto death, and was numbered with the transgressors. For he bore the sin of many, and made intercession for the transgressors* (Isaiah 53:12).

As the high priest interceded for the sinner, so is Christ *sitting at the place of highest honor next to God, pleading for us there in heaven* (Romans 8:34, TLB).

As the priest washed the sins of the people away in the bronze laver, so Jesus washes His church...

> *...to make her holy and clean, washed by baptism and God's Word; so that he could give her to himself as a glorious church without a single spot or wrinkle or any other blemish, being holy and without a single fault.*
>
> —Ephesians 5:26–27, TLB

As Aaron wore a mitre on his head, so Jesus was *crowned ... with glory and honor* (Hebrews 2:7, TLB). As the gold plate said, *"Consecrated to Jehovah,"* so our Lord was set apart and sanctified for us.

As the priest was chosen from among men...

> *...it was necessary for Jesus to be like us, his brothers, so that he could be our merciful and faithful High Priest before God, a Priest who would be both merciful to us and faithful to God in dealing with the sins of the people.*
>
> —Hebrews 2:17, TLB

As Moses anointed Aaron with oil made from a secret recipe never to be duplicated, so the Holy Spirit anoints us for Christian service.

Peter stated:

> *"And you no doubt know that Jesus of Nazareth was anointed by God with the Holy Spirit and with power, and he went around doing good and healing all who were possessed by demons, for God was with him."*
>
> —Acts 10:38, TLB

As Moses put the sacrificial blood of the ram on the priests' right ears, thumbs, and big toes, so we in dedication to our Lord should constantly listen for His voice even in the midst of daily noise and confusion; we should serve and encourage others with our hands; and we should walk in the courtyard of our God, following the path in which He leads.

> *God was patient with them forty years, though they tried his patience sorely; he kept right on doing his mighty miracles for them to see. "But," God says, "I was very angry with them, for their hearts were always looking somewhere else instead of up to me, and they never found the paths I wanted them to follow."*
>
> —Hebrews 3:9–10, TLB

O God, may we be faithful in finding the paths You want us to follow!

> *Moses did a fine job working in God's house, but he was only a servant; and his work was mostly to illustrate and suggest those things that would happen later on. But Christ, God's faithful Son, is in complete charge of God's house. And we Christians are God's house — he lives in us! — if we keep up our courage firm to the end, and our joy and our trust in the Lord.*
>
> —Hebrews 3:5–6, TLB

Today we don't go to the Holy Place, but we can bring the needs of others to the Lord in prayer; for as Peter says, we are a royal priesthood:

> *You have been chosen by God himself — you are priests of the King, you are holy and pure, you are God's very own — all this so that you may show to others how God called you out of the darkness into his wonderful light.*
>
> —1 Peter 2:9, TLB

Consulting the Map

Intercession is not a word used commonly in the English language today; let's take a look at what it means. The *International Standard Bible Encyclopedia* defines it this way:

> Intercession is prayer on behalf of another, and naturally arises from the instinct of the human heart — not merely prompted by affection and interest, but recognizing that God's relation to man is not merely individual, but social.[1]

Look up the following verses and note what each says about prayer on behalf of another.

1 Samuel 12:23

_____

Job 42:10

_____

Matthew 5:44

_____

Romans 15:30

_____

2 Corinthians 1:11

_____

Ephesians 6:18

_____

1 Timothy 2:1

_____

Rest Stop

As you see, we are called to pray for one another. Is God bringing a particular person to your mind right now — a friend or a foe? Take a moment to pray for that person regarding whatever it is that God has brought to your mind. Write your prayer here.

_____

_____

_____

_____

_____

_____

_____

In review, God chose Aaron as the high priest to go between the guilty man in need of cleansing and God Himself. As the high priest went before God, he brought the name of the sinners, who were then forgiven.

In New Testament times, God chose His Son Jesus as our leader, as the intercessor for us. As our High Priest, Jesus brings our needs before the Father. He is our go-between when we wish to enter the Holy Place and stand before God.

By following the steps of our High Priest, we will come into the presence of God:

> *Yes, the old system of priesthood based on family lines was canceled because it didn't work. It was weak and useless for saving people. It never made anyone really right with God. But now we have a far better hope, for Christ makes us acceptable to God, and now we may draw near to him.*
>
> —Hebrews 7:18–19, TLB

Let us follow our Leader and be cleansed.

Trip Journal

1. How logical it is to think that God only chooses godly people to do His work; yet, how obvious it is in the Bible that God chooses unlikely souls. Can you think of any Christian leaders whose backgrounds, education, and training did not fit what we assume to be the norm? What is God's requisite for leadership? How do you prepare to become a leader? What is the difference between leadership and servanthood?

2. How can we be mirrors that reflect God's glory? According to 2 Corinthians 3:18, what works inside us to institute change in our lives? What can you do personally to become more like the Lord?

3. What does the word *confess* really mean? How is it used in 1 John 1:9? We've seen how Moses cleansed the priests; how does God cleanse us today?

4. Do you feel God has put a "call" on your life? What causes you to sense this call? What do you think God is calling you to do? Are you willing to let Him have His way? Why or why not?

5. What was significant about Aaron's wearing on his shoulders the two stones with twelve names engraved on them? How does this compare with our keeping a prayer list today?

6. What is an *intercessor?* How is this term used to apply to the high priest of the Old Testament? To Jesus? To us? How often do you intercede for others? What method do you use to remind yourself to pray? Why was the old method of choosing the high priest discontinued? (See Hebrews 7:18–19.)

For Your Notebook

Add to your list of sevens:

    Aaron's seven items of clothing

    Seven days of dedication

    Seven days in our week

Make a comparison chart of Aaron the high priest and Jesus the Great High Priest. The following list will help get you started.

AARON	**JESUS**
Called of God	Called of God
Atonement made by blood of goat	Atonement made by His own blood

You might be interested in looking up the history of the twelve birthstones for each month of the year and copying these into your notebook. Do you feel there is any connection between these and the stones sewed into the high priest's garments?

Enter the Holy Place — And See the Light

Review Exodus 25:31–40; 37:17–24.

So far on our journey we have traveled out of the garden, into the fields, through the rain, and into a prison. We have come out of Egypt and gone through the wilderness. We have dwelt in the desert, and sought the Lord where He may be found. We've entered into His gates with praise, and have paid the price of sacrifice. We have met the priest at the altar, followed his instructions, and been washed in the water.

We are now ready to enter the Holy Place; inside this tent covered with skins is a lampstand shedding light, a table of shewbread, and an altar of incense. But in the Old Testament tabernacle, only the high priest was allowed inside. How can we enter into the presence of God?

> *One thing have I desired of the LORD, that will I seek after; that I may dwell in the house of the LORD all the days of my life, to behold the beauty of the LORD, and to enquire in his temple.*
>
> —Psalm 27:4, KJV

For God's People in Bible Times

In the days of the tabernacle, anyone could enter into the courtyard as long as he brought a sacrifice, but only the priest could enter the Holy Place. While the outside gate through the linen fence was wide enough for all to enter, the door into the sanctuary was narrow. That is, it was only for the priests, those who had been anointed, cleansed, and made ready to stand in the house of the Lord.

Consulting the Map

Though many were able to enter into the tabernacle, only a few experienced the presence of God inside the Holy Place.

How does Jesus describe Himself in John 10:9?

_____

According to John 14:6, how do we gain access to God?

_____

The door is narrow and difficult to enter. The road is narrow and contains obstacles. Read the following verses and note what we may stumble upon when walking the narrow road that leads to God's presence.

Proverbs 4:26–27

_____

Acts 14:22

_____

According to Matthew 16:24–25, what must we be willing to do in order to walk the narrow road?

_____

The narrow road and the wide road are diametrically opposite. Jesus will lead us down the narrow road, but Satan entices us to choose the wide path. Read John 10:10 and explain the contrast between these two potential "leaders."

_____

_____

_____

The wide road is the easy road, the one most traveled, the one with the most people, but it leads to destruction. The narrow road may be difficult, but that's where we'll find satisfaction and abundant life.

The outside of the tent may have been plain and unappealing, but the moment the priest stepped inside, he was awed by the beauty and majesty of his surroundings. In the courtyard the furnishings were bronze; in the Holy Place they were gold. Inside, the light from the golden lampstand cast a shadow over the gold-crowned table of the shewbread. And the sweet-smelling incense wafted a welcome aroma. Once inside, the priest was to keep the incense burning, to trim the wicks on the oil lamps, and to eat the bread put before him.

No doubt the priests had whispered about the spectacular sights to be seen in the sanctuary, and everyone wished they could catch a glimpse of the grandeur. But the ordinary person had no hope of entering the Holy Place; he could only look upon the outside of the tent and imagine what it would be like.

The first item the priest saw as he entered was the gold lampstand. This was not a candelabra designed for wax candles such as those we have today; rather, it was a stand that held oil and wicks. Beaten out from one piece of pure gold, it had a central shaft and three curved arms out of each side.

The lampstand was ornately decorated with almond buds, and the seven cups were almond blossoms. This use of buds and flowers showed that God's light was alive and growing. The almond was chosen because it was the first tree in bloom in the spring and because it represented new life, new growth, and resurrection. The meaning of the word *almond* was "wait and watch."[1]

For Us in Today's World

Based on our own good works or righteousness, we cannot enter into the Holy Place any more than the Hebrew could. But we can come to God because of our High Priest, Jesus Christ. We come into the Holy Place of God's presence on Christ's recommendation, as He declares us to be *a chosen people, a royal priesthood ... called out of darkness into his wonderful light"* (1 Peter 2:9).

Not everyone is able to come into God's presence in this way — only those who have given their lives to Jesus will be able to enter:

"Enter through the narrow gate. For wide is the gate and broad is the road that leads to destruction, and many enter through it. But small is the gate and narrow the road that leads to life, and only a few find it."

—Matthew 7:13–14

To many nonbelievers, the Christian life is not an attractive prospect. They often have the impression that it is a life filled only with legalism, piety, and sacrifice. But just as the tabernacle was covered with skins belying the beauty inside, so the true treasures to be found in Christ become apparent only after we have chosen to enter into His glorious presence. Only through the reflected light of the believer's life can the world catch a glimpse of what awaits inside the narrow gate. As Paul instructed the Christians:

Do all things without murmurings and disputings: That ye may be blameless and harmless, the sons of God, without rebuke, in the midst of a crooked and perverse nation, among whom ye shine as lights in the world.

—Philippians 2:14–15, KJV

Consulting the Map

The lampstand in the tabernacle was the only source of illumination; yet its light allowed those who entered the Holy Place to see the other articles in the temple. Without the lampstand there would have been only darkness.

How does Jesus describe Himself in John 9:5?

_____

According to John 3:19–21, what happened when the light came into the world?

_____

Explain the promise Christ gave in John 8:12 to those who follow Him.

_____

_____

How does Matthew 5:14 describe the church?

_____

According to Ephesians 5:8, how should we walk out the Christian life? How does this relate to being "a city set on a hill"?

_____

_____

Are we living in a crooked and perverse nation today? How important it is that we provide illumination, that we shine as lights in the world! You may be the only glimpse of Jesus that your neighbor will ever see.

If we are to be lights in the world, we must be pure and of one mind, just as the gold of the lampstand was of one piece with no alloys or soldering. As believers, we are branches who are united in one vine — Jesus Christ — just as the branches of the lampstand were connected to one central shaft.

Jesus Himself said clearly, _"I am the vine; you are the branches. If a man remains in me and I in him, he will bear much fruit; apart from me you can do nothing"_ (John 15:5).

When I think of the beaten gold of the lampstand, I'm reminded of the suffering Jesus was to go through, as well as the trials we as believers have to face:

> _In this you greatly rejoice, though now for a little while you may have had to suffer grief in all kinds of trials. These have come so that your faith — of greater worth than gold, which perishes even though refined by fire — may be proved genuine and may result in praise, glory and honor when Jesus Christ is revealed._
>
> —1 Peter 1:6–7

Consulting the Map

According to James 1:2, what are we exhorted to do when faced with trials?

_____

According to James 1:3–4, what reasons do we have for "counting them as joy"?

_____

According to 1 Peter 4:12–13, what can believers expect, and what hope can we gain in spite of it?

_____

The golden lampstand in the temple was made from a talent of gold — worth as much as $30,000 today. How does 1 Peter 1:6–7 describe our faith?

———————————————————————————————————

Rest Stop

Based on the verses above, write a prayer asking the Lord to refine you as necessary, and work in you a faith that's pure, worth more than gold.

———————————————————————————————————

———————————————————————————————————

———————————————————————————————————

———————————————————————————————————

Only when gold is refined by fire does it become a thing of beauty; only as we are tested and tried are we purified and sanctified unto His service. As the almond was chosen to represent new birth, so we only come into full flower for the Lord as we are born again into new life.

> *Praise be to the God and Father of our Lord Jesus Christ! In his great mercy he has given us new birth into a living hope through the resurrection of Jesus Christ from the dead.*
>
> —1 Peter 1:3

As the golden lampstand was the only light in the Holy Place, so is Jesus the only Light in a world of darkness: *In him was life, and that life was the light of men* (John 1:4).

In these dark days, people are looking for God as never before, but they don't want to accept the Light: *The light shines in the darkness, but the darkness has not understood it* (John 1:5).

In the book of Revelation, John wrote, foretelling the future of the Christian church:

> *I turned around to see the voice that was speaking to me. And when I turned I saw seven golden lampstands, and among the lampstands was someone "like a son of man" dressed in a robe reaching down to his feet and with a golden sash around his chest.... His face was like the sun shining in all its brilliance.*
>
> —Revelation 1:12–13, 16

Jesus, our High Priest, will come again, and be the Light of our dark, evil world: *There will be no more night. They will not need the light of a lamp or the light of the sun, for the Lord God will give them light. And they will reign for ever and ever* (Revelation 22:5).

As the priests of the past stood in the light of the lampstand, Jesus our High Priest provides the light for each believer today and in the future. He'll come again as the Light of the world, and He will reign forever and ever. To find our God, we must first see the light of Jesus.

Scenic Overlook

After sitting at a table writing all day, I went out to the Jacuzzi at the motel to relax my right arm and back. There I met a pleasant Canadian couple, Carl and Sue, who were on vacation, and we began to talk. When they asked what I was doing, I explained that I wrote Christian books, and I needed a short break from my work. I told them about *Journey to Jesus,* and Carl replied, "I'm a Christian, but just recently I met God on a new level." He then told me of a dream he'd had in which he had been walking down a road at dusk. Lights began to come on and he could see the city straight ahead. As he trudged along, the stars began to shine and the moon came over a mountain.

Suddenly, everything went black, and he was alone in the darkness. Flames licked up around his feet for a fleeting moment, and then they died away. There were no light, no stars, no moon, no shadows, no people, and no sound. He screamed for help, but there was no response. He demanded light but the answer was darkness. Soon he realized he was in hell.

"Where are the flames?" he called out. "I thought hell was full of fire." There was no answer, only total darkness, an utter absence of any tiny ray of light.

Then he cried out to God, "Father, forgive me! I'll do anything You say if You'll take me out of the darkness into the light. Show me light; give me hope!"

As Carl repeated this to me, he said he had woken up crying, and for the first time he realized what God's Word meant when it said, *The Lord is my light and my salvation — whom shall I fear?* (Psalm 27:1).

When God spoke to the Hebrew people about their disobedience and deception, He explained that if they didn't mend their ways they would be punished:

The LORD will afflict you with madness, blindness, and confusion of mind. At midday you will grope about like a blind man in the dark. You will be unsuccessful in everything you do; day after day you will be oppressed and robbed, with no one to rescue you.

—Deuteronomy 28:28–29

The absence of light is an affliction of the Lord, a groping in the dark, the way of the wicked. As we discussed this concept of darkness in the hot California sun, Carl concluded, "I've believed in God forever, but I hadn't fully understood the necessity of Jesus' saying, 'I am the light of the world. Whoever follows Me will never walk in darkness, but will have the light of life.'"

Carl groped for God in a dream of darkness and found Him in a new light.

LESSON 20

Eat the Bread — And Give Thanks

Review Exodus 25:23–30 and 37:10–16.

As we stand in the light, we can see the table of shewbread before us. Now that we're here, may we partake of this bread "frosted" in frankincense? Is it for us? If so, what are we to do with it?

For God's People in Bible Times

Once inside the Holy Place, standing in the ever-present light, the high priest could see before him the table of shewbread. Built somewhat like a piano bench, the table was made of acacia wood overlaid with gold. There was a gold edging along the outside perimeter to keep the bread from falling off of the table when it was being moved throughout the desert (see Exodus 25:24). The twelve loaves of bread made of fine flour represented the twelve tribes of Israel. No matter how big or small the tribe, they all had the same size loaf, showing that numbers are not necessarily important to God.

Consulting the Map

The twelve loaves of bread on the table represented each of the twelve tribes of Israel. The Hebrew definition for the word *table* is "a place of eating."[1] It carries with it the idea of a gathering of individuals for a time of food and fellowship — a place of unconditional love and acceptance.

Look up the following scriptures and note what kinds of people shared a table with Jesus.

Luke 5:27–35

Luke 22:14

_____

John 12:1–2

_____

Read the account of King David and Mephibosheth in 2 Samuel 9, and then answer the following questions.

Why did King David invite Mephibosheth to his table?

_____

What was wrong with Mephibosheth?

_____

How did Mephibosheth view himself?

_____

In what manner did Mephibosheth eat at King David's table?

_____

How long was Mephibosheth welcome at King David's table?

_____

To be invited to sit at a king's table would be considered a great honor. Read Luke 22:29–30. Who has invited us to sit at His table in His kingdom?

_____

The _International Standard Bible Encyclopedia_ states, "In large households such as those of a king, those that ate at the table were members of the household."[2] Read Romans 8:14–17 and explain why we have been invited to sit at the King's table.

_____

_____

_____

In _The Tabernacle of Moses_, Kevin Conner states that the table of shewbread had both a godly and a human side: the gold represented God, and the wood, humanity. The bread stood for

God's provision for this people: *Let them give thanks to the* Lord *for his unfailing love and his wonderful deeds for men, for he satisfies the thirsty and fills the hungry with good things* (Psalm 107:8–9).

Bread has always been considered the staff of life, the most basic of foods. When the Hebrews were hungry in the desert, God provided manna, a sticky white bread that appeared mysteriously in abundance each day for forty years. The phrase *"Give us this day our daily bread"* (Matthew 6:11, KJV) later became part of the Lord's model prayer. Bread was so significant in the sustenance of the Hebrews in the wilderness that a jar of manna was one of the three items placed in the ark of the covenant, along with Aaron's rod and the tablets of Moses, to give a remembrance of God's perpetual provision for man's needs.

The *shewbread,* literally "bread of presence,"[3] was frosted with frankincense, a sweet-smelling white gum signifying purity, and placed on the table by the priests as an ever-present display before God. Since each tribe was represented, God could see a symbol of His people in the "presence bread," sometimes called "continual bread," and could feast on the fellowship of His believers forever. Not only was the bread of spiritual significance to be a constant memorial and a presence, but it was also to be food for the priests. As part of his ritual, the high priest was to change the bread once a week: *Every sabbath he shall set it in order before the* Lord *continually* (Leviticus 24:8, KJV).

God was given the fresh new bread, and the twelve loaves that were removed became the bread for the priests that week. They ate the Bread of God; they partook of God's presence; they entered into communion with their God.

For Us in Today's World

As the shewbread was a memorial of God's provision and His presence, so our Lord Jesus asks us to take the sacred bread of communion in remembrance of Him (see Luke 22:19).

Consulting the Map

Read Luke 22:17–20.

What is the purpose of the Lord's Supper? (verse 19)

_____

_____

What was the first thing Christ did when He took the cup? (verse 17)

_____

What did the cup symbolize? (verse 20)

_____

What was the first thing Jesus did when He took the bread? (verse 19)

_____

What did the bread symbolize? (verse 19)

_____

According to 1 Corinthians 11:26, how long are we to continue taking communion?

_____

Rest Stop

Take time right now to write a prayer of thanks to Jesus Christ for giving His body and blood for you.

_____

_____

_____

_____

_____

For years, the Passover Feast reminded God's people to look to the past and remember their deliverance from Egypt — as well as look forward to the coming of the Savior. Christ commands us as well to remember the Cross — until the day He comes again.

Just as the presence bread was to be before God at all times, so is Jesus, our "Bread of Life," available to us moment by moment, so that we may continually feed our souls with His spiritual nourishment: _"I am the bread of life. He who comes to me will never go hungry"_ (John 6:35); _"I am the living bread that came down from heaven. If anyone eats of this bread, he will live forever. This bread is my flesh, which I will give for the life of the world"_ (John 6:51); _"This is the bread that came down from heaven. Your forefathers ate manna and died, but he who feeds on this bread will live forever"_ (John 6:58).

Jesus Himself told us that we need spiritual food, and He is our Bread; He will sustain us. As the priests ate holy bread, so can we receive strength from our own High Priest. As the priests in the tabernacle ate the shewbread in fellowship with God, so Jesus wants His disciples to have communion with Him: *"Is not the bread that we break a participation in the body of Christ?"* (1 Corinthians 10:16).

Instead of twelve loaves, Jesus presented Himself to God as one loaf. No longer are we to think of God's people as from different tribes or backgrounds, but we become a united body in Christ: *Because there is one loaf, we, who are many, are one body, for we all partake of the one loaf* (1 Corinthians 10:17).

When Paul gave instructions for the Lord's Supper, he told the Corinthians they were first to examine their lives:

> *For whenever you eat this bread and drink this cup, you proclaim the Lord's death until he comes. Therefore, whoever eats the bread or drinks the cup of the Lord in an unworthy manner will be guilty of sinning against the body and blood of the Lord. A man ought to examine himself before he eats of the bread and drinks of the cup. For anyone who eats and drinks without recognizing the body of the Lord eats and drinks judgment on himself.*
>
> —1 Corinthians 11:26–29

Then Paul added a personal and pointed explanation: *That is why many among you are weak and sick, and a number of you have fallen asleep!* (1 Corinthians 11:30).

For us today, Paul's words still hold true: We're sick and tired of living because we have not examined ourselves before God, we have not given thanks for what we do have, and we have not eaten of the Bread of Life for our spiritual sustenance.

Jesus is our daily Bread, fresh every morning. When we eat of Him, we will be strengthened, we will have joy, and we will live forever.

Consulting the Map

According to Exodus 16:21, when did God provide the manna from heaven?

_____

Read Exodus 16:12. When were God's people to eat the bread He had provided for them?

_____

The bread that God provided for His people in the morning gave them strength for the day. *Barnes' Notes on the New Testament* says: "This will be found to be true, universally, that the religious enjoyment through the day will be according to the state of the heart in the morning; and can, therefore be measured by our faithfulness in early secret prayer."[4]

The Bible gives us many examples of those who began their day seeking the Lord. Read the verses below to discover who some of those people were.

Genesis 19:27

_____

Genesis 28:18

_____

Judges 6:38–39

_____

2 Chronicles 29:20

_____

Job 1:5

_____

Mark 1:35

_____

David was called "the man after God's own heart." Read the following verses and note what you learn about his heart for seeking the Lord in the morning.

Psalm 5:3

_____

Psalm 88:13

_____

Psalm 119:147

_____

Psalm 143:8

_____

Read Matthew 6:32–33. Why does it make sense for us to begin our day seeking the Lord?

_____

_____

Barnes' Notes on the New Testament encourages us to seek the Lord "before the world gets possession of our thoughts; before Satan fills us with unholy feelings; when we rise fresh from beds of repose, and while the world around us is still!"[5] We're not to stop seeking the Lord after meeting with Him in the morning, however; we should continue throughout the day.

What does Joshua 1:8 instruct us to do with God's Word day and night?

_____

How do we "eat" of Jesus each day? There are two kinds of nourishment: physical and spiritual. There are few of us who do not get enough food each day. Since overeating is considered a chronic American health problem, we don't need to be encouraged to physically eat more, but many of us need to be challenged to feed more on God's Word, our spiritual food. There is no way we can grow spiritually if we are not daily reading the Word and spending time in God's presence.

Moses explained this to his people:

> *"He humbled you, causing you to hunger and then feeding you with manna, which neither you nor your fathers had known, to teach you that man does not live on bread alone but on every word that comes from the mouth of the LORD."*
>
> —Deuteronomy 8:3

Job declared, *"I have treasured the words of his mouth more than my daily bread"* (Job 23:12). The psalmist wrote: *The law from your mouth is more precious to me than thousands of pieces of silver and gold.... How sweet are your words to my taste, sweeter than honey to my mouth!* (Psalm 119:72, 103). Jeremiah also loved God's Word: *When your words came, I ate them: they were my joy and my heart's delight* (Jeremiah 15:16).

When I first hungered after the Lord, I spent six hours or, more each day in study. Had I spent that much time physically eating, I would have been bulging; instead, I was filled up on God's Word. As Peter wrote, *Like newborn babies, crave pure spiritual milk, so that by it you may grow up in your salvation* (1 Peter 2:2).

Often I hear women say, "I wish I knew the Bible better," or, "I wish I could use the Scriptures the way that you do." When this happens, I ask them, "How much time do you spend each week in study?" We all want to be spiritual giants quickly. We would like to have instant Bible knowledge as easily as we can have instant potatoes, but to know God well and to grow in His Word, we must spend time studying joyfully for nourishment.

Paul wrote, *The word is near you; it is in your mouth and in your heart* (Romans 10:8); *For everything that was written in the past was written to teach us, so that through endurance and the encouragement of the Scriptures we might have hope* (Romans 15:4).

Just as the priests ate of the bread of the presence, so we will taste of the presence of our Lord Jesus as we eat daily of His Word and give thanks.

Scenic Overlook

A few years ago I spoke at a meeting where I was introduced to Beth, a lawyer's wife. The minute I met her, I knew she was special. We became long-distance friends, and each time I'd go to her city, I'd call her up. She would always be amazed that I remembered her and flattered that I found her a fun friend to be with. She heard my testimony many times and agreed that we all needed to "find God." Beth was a good person who went to church faithfully and had even minored in theology in college. She would frequently remind me of these facts so I would know she was "spiritual," even though I never pushed her for any commitment. I just interceded; I just carried her quietly before the Lord.

When we took our Christian leadership seminar to her city, she attended because she felt she "owed it" to me. In the small group session on the first day, she was amazed at how open and honest the people were. She reported, "They don't seem to care what the others think of them." Later she told me she couldn't sleep at all that night. She paced the floor and wrestled with God as Jacob had, although she didn't realize what was taking place. On the second day of the seminar, she went home before the small groups convened. She couldn't face the open vulnerability — she was trying to "keep it all together."

On the third day, she was surprised that the small groups were meeting before lunch, and she was trapped into going. She was dumbfounded that "ordinary people" could take a Bible verse and make it apply to their lives, while she, who had minored in theology, couldn't. "I don't know what's wrong with me," she cried, as we sat together at lunch. "I'm an intelligent person. I've studied religion, but I don't know what to do with one simple verse. I just came to the seminar to please you. I didn't know this whole thing was going to get like this. What's happening to me? Why are my insides all fluttering and shaky?" As I explained that God was working in her life, she said, "You've had your eye on me right from the first time we met, haven't you?"

At that moment, one of our staff members, Patsy Clairmont, got up to give a lunch talk about humor in speaking. She explained how humor can be a great asset in speaking, but we must always be sure it leads to a point. At the conclusion of her talk, Beth said, "I'm just as funny as Patsy. I make people laugh all the time, but I haven't found anything productive to do with my humor."

"Do your stories have a point?" I asked.

"That's the problem," she added quickly. "That's the problem with my life. It's full of funny things, but it doesn't have a point."

By this time everyone had left the lunchroom to return to the seminar where I was due to begin teaching, yet I couldn't leave Beth at this critical moment. Suddenly I saw Patsy and called her over. "Beth has a sense of humor just like yours, Patsy, but she needs you to show her how to bring it to a point." Patsy did bring Beth's life to a point. She told her the tremors in her stomach were labor pains preparing her for a new birth, and that her minor in theology did not mean that she had been born into the family of God. As I spoke in the sanctuary, Patsy birthed Beth as a babe in Christ.

LESSON 21

Smell the Aroma —
And Worship God

Review Exodus 30:1–5; 37:25–-29.

Can you believe we're almost at the end of our journey? We've been through gardens and deserts, on mountains and in valleys. We've followed the map and collected baskets of memories we'll never forget. We've been allowed to enter the Holy Place reserved only for the priests. We've seen the Light, and we've eaten the Bread with thankful hearts. But what is the aroma we smell? Where is it coming from? Let's find out.

For God's People in Bible Times

As you may recall, in the outer court of the tabernacle stood the bronze altar of sacrifice, a place of continual bloodshed. But in the Holy Place, there was built an altar of gold, where the sweet aroma of incense was constantly wafting toward heaven. This altar of incense also was bordered with a crown of gold, signifying the glory of God.

The incense, like the oil of consecration, was made from a special recipe of four spices chosen by God Himself. Anyone duplicating it for his own pleasure would be excommunicated — kept from fellowship with God. How it must grieve our Father today as He sees so many making their own recipes for worship, taking part of His divine plan, but rejecting His power; sounding saintly, but following false gods.

The holy perfume was to be burning constantly: *Aaron must burn fragrant incense on the altar every morning when he tends the lamps. He must burn incense again when he lights the lamps at twilight so incense will burn regularly before the LORD for the generations to come* (Exodus 30:7–8).

The aroma ascending to God was to be constant, not just a thing of the moment. David wrote, *May my prayer be set before you like incense; may the lifting up of my hands be like the evening sacrifice* (Psalm 141:2).

The altar of incense was the last object the priest passed before entering into the Holy of Holies, the very presence of God. Without first offering prayers and praise, the priest couldn't come to the Lord.

Consulting the Map

Praise is an important part of our worship of God, a sweet aroma wafting to heaven. Let's look at God's Word to see what the Scriptures say about praise — and then let's look at our lives to determine if we are actively involved in praise.

Read the following scriptures. First, note the different elements given in each verse and then determine if this is an area in which you need to improve.

(Hint: In Scripture, when the word *bless* is used in reference to blessing the Lord, it is synonymous with praise: "When men bless God ... they ascribe to Him those characteristics that are His, acknowledge His sovereignty, express gratitude for His mercies, etc."[1])

1 Chronicles 29:20

_____

2 Chronicles 5:13

_____

Nehemiah 9:5

_____

Psalm 9:11

_____

Psalm 33:2

_____

Psalm 35:28

_____

Psalm 67:3

_____

Acts 16:25

_____

Hebrews 13:15

_____

Make a commitment to incorporate whatever elements of praise are not a part of your life into your daily worship with God.

For Us in Today's World

As we learned earlier, the altar of sacrifice represents the cross on which Christ gave up His life for us. Likewise, the altar of incense represents the risen, glorified Christ who is interceding for us before the Father; His prayers continually produce a sweet-smelling aroma before the throne. How grateful we should be that Christ didn't just say, *"It is finished"* (John 19:30), and then disappear, leaving us to our own problems. Instead, He is always praying on behalf of His believers, noticing our needs and pleading our case before the Judge. Jesus is our *golden altar before the throne* (Revelation 8:3).

Consulting the Map

In lesson 18 we learned of our responsibility to intercede in prayer for others. Now let's look at how Jesus intercedes for us.

Have you ever wanted to "connect" in some way with someone important whom you did not know? Maybe you wanted to get an autograph from that person or give them some kind of gift because of their impact on your life. Imagine that you do not know that person. You do not know how to reach them — but you know someone who does. You would go to that friend and ask them to approach the other person on your behalf.

That is what Jesus does for us. He knows His Father well and on our behalf, He brings our concerns to His Father.

Read the following verses and note the specifics of Jesus' prayers for us.

Luke 22:32

_____

Luke 23:34

_____

John 14:16

_____

John 17:9

_____

Romans 8:34

_____

Rest Stop

Does it bring comfort when you know that a fellow Christian is praying for you? How much greater that sense of security should be when we know Jesus prays on our behalf! How wonderful to know that Jesus prays for all of humanity, for the body of believers (His Church), and for each of us as individuals — even today. Take a few moments and write a prayer of thanks to Jesus for His prayers to the Father for you.

_____

_____

_____

_____

As the incense burned on the altar and ascended to God, so our prayers begin in our hearts and rise to heaven when we pray in the power of our Intercessor — when we pray "in Jesus' name." Just as this altar stood in the way of entrance into God's presence, so we are hindered in our search for Him when we do not pray.

Paul wrote, _Be joyful always; pray continually; give thanks in all circumstances, for this is God's will for you in Christ Jesus. Do not put out the Spirit's fire_ (1 Thessalonians 5:16–19). Don't let the incense of your prayers burn out. Tend it in the morning and in the night. *Pray in the Spirit on all occasions with all kinds of prayers and requests. With this in mind, be alert and always keep on praying for all the saints* (Ephesians 6:18).

We must be alert and not allow the fire within us to go out. We don't want to be lukewarm Christians whose pitiful prayers never go above our heads. The Jesus of Revelation said, *"I know your deeds, that you are neither cold nor hot. I wish you were either one or the other! So, because you are lukewarm — neither hot nor cold — I am about to spit you out of my mouth"* (Revelation 3:15–16).

Consulting the Map

A Christian whose fire has gone out is referred to in Scripture as "lukewarm." Clearly, this is a problem. How does one become lukewarm? How does one change from being lukewarm to being on fire for God?

Read the following scripture passages, and note how each further defines the problem of being lukewarm.

1 Samuel 15:11

_____

2 Chronicles 12:1

_____

Hosea 6:4

_____

Jonah 1:3

_____

Revelation 2:4

_____

Revelation 3:2

_____

Read the following scripture passages, and note the solutions each provides for the problem of being lukewarm.

Deuteronomy 6:5

_____

Deuteronomy 11:13

_____

2 Chronicles 31:21

_____

Matthew 12:30

_____

Mark 12:30

_____

Luke 10:27

_____

Like a parent speaking to a child, God often repeats things for us before we "catch it."

Why do you think that is? What does the repetition in the verses listed above tell you?

_____

_____

How many of us are constantly looking for God but are not serious enough about our search to make the necessary sacrifices? We're not bad people with cold hearts; we're just not hot after God's program. We're lukewarm believers, and God is ready to spit us out.

If we've come this far and we're standing just a few steps from God's presence, what do we need to do to get His attention? As the incense wafted up to the Lord and pleased Him, so we must pray without ceasing that He will hear our voice, a voice that may be crying in the wilderness: _Be imitators of God, therefore, as dearly loved children and live a life of love, just as Christ loved us and gave himself up for us as a fragrant offering and sacrifice to God_ (Ephesians

5:1–2). Let's give up our tepid trust in a nebulous God and become burning incense whose aroma reaches into the very nostrils of our heavenly Father.

Once lit, how do we keep the fire going? Many Christians seem to be dedicated to good works but they have a lukewarm prayer life. They have had instructions in all kinds of godly pursuits, but somehow they've missed the importance of communicating with God.

After I had taught Bible studies in our women's club for years, I decided it was time I taught them to pray. I announced that the following week we would divide into small groups, and I'd lead them in simple sentence prayers. The next week only one-third of the regular attendance showed up! They liked listening to me and getting their spirituality secondhand, but they didn't want to be involved if they had to take any risks. What if they didn't pray right? What would people think?

The Lord doesn't want pretty little prayers designed to impress others. He wants us to send up fervent prayers, heated prayers — prayers strong enough to reach Him: *The effectual fervent prayer of a righteous man availeth much* (James 5:16, KJV).

Christians can compare calling on God in prayer to calling a friend on the phone. Everyone knows how to use a phone. Everyone knows that in a time of trouble, you should reach out and call someone. For us, God's phone number is JER–3303 (Jeremiah 33:3): *Call to me and I will answer you and tell you great and unsearchable things you do not know.* God is never too busy; He's always at home; His number is available; and Jesus is our Operator, our Intercessor, our connection with the heavenly mansion. God is a God of clear circuits, and as we pray without ceasing, He will hear and answer.

Do you want to find God? Give Him a call. He's waiting to give you an answer.

So often our prayers are for ourselves: "Help me, God. I'm in trouble again." As Jesus became our example in prayer, He showed us how to pray for others — how to be an intercessor for others as He is for us.

When we intercede in prayer, as we learned in lesson 18, we literally go between the person in need and our God. We become a willing body, a bridge over troubled waters, bringing our friend and his burdens from wherever he is into the presence of God. In essence, we're saying, "Here he is, God. I care enough about this person to bring him from the desert heat into the protective tent of Your presence." Likewise, we can ask others to lift us up in prayer.

Oswald Chambers wrote, "In intercession you bring the person, or the circumstance that impinges on you before God until you are moved by His attitude toward that person or circumstance."[2]

The reason so few of us become intercessors is that there's no credit connected with lifting up a heavy burden daily in the confines of our closet. Platform evangelism is a showcase for God's power through us — we get to be seen by an audience, and it gives us the feeling that God is proud of our humble harvest. We imagine some heavenly wall of granite with the names of our converts carved in stone, much like the Vietnam Memorial. Although there's no public recognition for those who prayed, planted seeds in, and watered these prospects up to the point of their conversion, God sees those who lift up their friends in faith before His face. What He sees us do in secret, He will reward openly.

Consulting the Map

Read John 4:35–38.
What does this passage say about the person who does the behind-the-scenes work, who sows the seeds that ultimately lead someone to Christ?

_____

Regardless of our involvement, how should we respond when a person invites Jesus into their heart? Read the following verses and note your conclusion.

Acts 15:3

_____

Philippians 2:14–18

_____

As the high priest interceded between man and God, so Jesus is our Intercessor. We should follow His example, constantly uplifting our friends in prayer: _Admit your faults to one another and pray for each other so that you may be healed. The earnest prayer of a righteous man has great power and wonderful results_ (James 5:16, TLB).

Our earnest prayers waft as incense up to the heavenly Father. How He loves to smell the aroma as we worship Him in prayer. We can then feel His power and there will be wonderful results.

Scenic Overlook

Every year, the staff members in my organization each choose a verse to represent themselves on our prayer list. We all give our choices to one person on the team, who compiles them and returns a copy of all the verses to each one of us. With these selections in our hands, we can pray for each other using the scripture verse to personalize our prayers. One year, for example, I chose Philippians 3:10, giving me four clear aims for my Christian life: to get to know Christ; to feel the power of His resurrection; to share in His sufferings; and to become more like Him.

As each of the staff — including myself — prayed for me, keeping the words of this scripture in mind, I saw changes in the depth of my commitment to the Lord. During this time I also used Philippians 3:10 as the basis for a message to others, which I called "Aim and Action of the Christian Life."

Most amazing to me has been the reaction of audiences as I have mentioned this method of prayer support. To many, the thought of praying for each other through Scripture was a new idea. Many people came up and wanted to see the list of verses the staff had for each other. As I opened my organizer, they would peer at the names and verses and say happily, "Why, I could do that!" And of course they could, and you can, too.

One of the reasons people don't pray is they don't think they have anything to say. Even when alone, they're afraid God will think they're stupid if they don't have deep thoughts. Yet, when I show them how to personalize a verse and insert a friend's name, they often become quite eloquent.

I've received letters filled with excitement from women who confessed that their lukewarm prayer life had been reactivated when they found they could talk to God through a verse. One of these women sent me a copy of how she prayed daily for me using my verse, Philippians 3:10:

Lord, today I pray for Florence. I don't know where she is, but I pray for her according to Your Word. I ask that she get to know You better. To do that she'll have to spend more time with You. Give her the time today to study Your Word and learn of You as the perfect example for life. Lord, may she feel Your power. In the long days she puts in that would tire any of us, would You let her know that You are there: encouraging, strengthening, upholding her. Lord, as You suffered and as she has experienced grief, let her know that she is not alone, let her see the value in the trials of life to refine her character as into fine gold. Give her the joy to spread to others in need as she ministers to and comforts the afflicted. And most important, Lord, help her to keep her eyes on the goal: Jesus, the Author and the Finisher, Designer, Completer of her life, that she may one day become like You.

I pray this for Florence in faith, in hope, in love, and in Your name, the precious name of Jesus. Amen.

How easily the words flow in prayer when we are basing our requests firmly on God's Word! How grateful this lady was to go from a poor prayer life to an intimate relationship with God. Our God doesn't have an answering machine or a secretary; He takes every call Himself.

LESSON 22

Standing in the Presence of Jesus

Review Exodus 25:10–22; 37:1–9; 40:34–38.

We have arrived! In our journey to Jesus, we now stand at the very threshold of the Holy of Holies. As Jacob said, *"How awesome is this place! This is none other than the house of God; this is the gate of heaven"* (Genesis 28:17).

We have come a long way from the Garden of Eden, and we're ready to stand in the presence of our God. What do you think we'll find as we go through the veil and into the Holy of Holies?

For God's People in Bible Times

Only once each year the high priest was allowed to go into the Holy of Holies and come into the very presence of God. God had said, *"There I will meet with thee, and I will commune with thee"* (Exodus 25:22, KJV). On that one day, the Day of Atonement, the high priest, wearing his special garments with the names of all the tribes on his shoulders, came before God to plead for the people.

To enter this special room, the priest had to go through the veil that separated the two chambers. This curtain, embroidered with cherubim, was woven of fine linen in the three colors used throughout the tabernacle: blue, red, and purple. The veil, representing separation, presented a barrier that blocked the entrance into the Holy of Holies. This curtain was hung by gold hooks onto four gold-covered wooden pillars.

As the high priest came into God's presence through the veil, he saw shining before him the ark of the covenant, a chest made of acacia wood overlaid with pure gold. What is an ark? The first ark mentioned in the Bible was Noah's, made of gopher wood, pitched within and without, and representing the preservation of people — the salvation of the human race. The second "ark" was the ark of reeds and tar made for the baby Moses to preserve his life and save him from being killed by the Pharaoh. The ark of the covenant was the third, and in this golden chest was preserved a jar of manna (the symbol of God's provision for His people), the tablets of the Law (symbolizing God's principles of behavior), and Aaron's rod (God's symbol of power and leadership).

This ark had a crown of gold around the top and a golden ring on each corner to hold the staves used in carrying the ark from place to place as God directed. The ark not only preserved what was inside, but its presence in time of battle saved the Israelites from defeat. Its presence at the Jordan parted the river and saved the people. Its presence at Jericho caused the walls to fall, and saved the Hebrews from destruction. Later, King Saul went to the ark for help. David made a special tent to house it, and Solomon installed the ark in the temple. Throughout the wanderings of the Israelites, the ark was considered the symbol of God, but Jeremiah predicted that in later years they would forget the ark:

> *"In those days, when your numbers have increased greatly in the land," declares the LORD, "men will no longer say, 'The ark of the covenant of the LORD.' It will never enter their minds or be remembered; it will not be missed, nor will another one be made."*
>
> —Jeremiah 3:16

The lid of the ark was crafted of pure gold, with a gold cherub at each end. It was called the *mercy seat,* the place where God would distribute mercy. The wings of the cherubim overshadowed the ark in a symbol of protection, their heads bowed down to look at the mercy seat. As the priest approached God's place of mercy and grace, he brought the blood of a sin offering and sprinkled it seven times on the seat. God, in His mercy, forgave the sins of all the people for yet another year.

David once called out to God, *"For you have been my refuge, a strong tower against the foe. I long to dwell in your tent forever and take refuge in the shelter of your wings"* (Psalm 61:3–4). Another time he wrote: *On my bed I remember you; I think of you through the watches of the night. Because you are my help, I sing in the shadow of your wings* (Psalm 63:6–7). David had seen the ark and knew God's mercy. He had experienced refuge and shelter in the shadow of His almighty wings.

Once a year the high priest came before the ark of the covenant and saw the cherubim on the mercy seat, but where was God? Was He on vacation? Was there no throne? As the high priest entered the Holy of Holies, he was struck, not by furniture and decorations, but by the brilliance of God's presence: *The glory of the LORD filled the Tabernacle* (Exodus 40:35, TLB).

For Us in Today's World

Had we lived in the days of Moses, we would not have been allowed to enter the Holy of Holies and come into the presence of God. Unless one of us became the high priest and gave insider information to the rest of us, we would have no idea what was inside the tent covered over with badger skins. We could guess and imagine, but we couldn't get close enough to know. We would be allowed to come through the gate into the courtyard, we could see the doorway into the Holy Place, but we couldn't even visualize the veil with its message of "No Admittance."

What has happened since that time to allow you and me to come into the presence of God? As we have seen, the tabernacle, with all its furnishings built to God's specifications, was a prototype of what Christ would become for us.

• The sinful Israelite had to come to the gate — Jesus is our Gate, our Door, our Way. No one comes to the Father but through Him.

• The Israelite had to bring a sacrificial lamb — Jesus is our Lamb, the Lamb of God, without blemish or spot.

• The Israelite had to meet the priest — Jesus is our High Priest who makes intercession for us.

• The Israelite saw the bronze laver of washing — Jesus has washed us clean in the water of regeneration.

• The priests cared for the lamps and saw the light — Jesus is the Light of the World.

• The priests presented and ate the bread — Jesus is the Bread of Life and His Word is as sweet as honey.

• The priests kept the incense burning — Jesus is our sweet-smelling aroma to the Father.

• Only the high priest went through the veil into the Holy of Holies — Jesus is the veil of the new covenant.

How exciting it is to be touched by the symbolism in the tabernacle, and how dramatic it is to see God's great plan brought to fruition in the life of His Son, our Lord Jesus!

As He is our Door, our Lamb, our High Priest, our Light, our Bread, our Incense, He is also the veil through which you and I can pass into the full presence of God.

> *Therefore, brothers, since we have confidence to enter the Most Holy Place by the blood of Jesus, by a new and living way opened for us through the curtain [veil], that is, his body, and since we have a great priest over the house of God, let us draw near to God with a sincere heart in full assurance of faith, having our hearts sprinkled to cleanse us from a guilty conscience and having our bodies washed with pure water.*
>
> —Hebrews 10:19–22

Here in these few verses, we see how our Jesus shed His blood for us, removed the veil that separated us from God, and became our great High Priest. He did all that so that we could draw near to God if we had a sincere heart. Only Jesus' blood cleanses us, and only the living water of Christ can wash away our sins.

Consulting the Map

Jesus' blood cleanses our guilty conscience, but once cleansed, how can we keep our conscience pure? Read the following scriptures to find the answer.

Romans 2:15	**Romans 9:1**	**2 Corinthians 1:12**
Hebrews 9:14	**Hebrews 10:22**	**Hebrews 13:18**

_____

_____

_____

On the day when Jesus was crucified, when He "gave up His spirit," the veil was ripped in two, and the door was opened. Although the tabernacle was no longer set in the desert, Herod's temple in Jerusalem had become God's residence, and it had been built with the same floor plan as God had given Moses. The high priest functioned under the same Law; the veil was still the barrier to the Holy of Holies. At the very moment of Jesus' death, a supernatural power tore the veil.

> *And when Jesus had cried out again in a loud voice, he gave up his spirit. At that moment the curtain of the temple was torn in two from top to bottom. The earth shook and the rocks split.*
>
> —Matthew 27:50–51

Not only did the curtain tear, but it was torn from top to bottom to show that it was a divine, not a human, transaction. At that same moment, the Old Testament rituals and sacrifices were fulfilled, and we entered the time of the New Testament.

> *For this reason Christ is the mediator of a new covenant, that those who are called may receive the promised eternal inheritance — now that he has died as a ransom to set them free from the sins committed under the first covenant.*
>
> —Hebrews 9:15

> *We have this hope as an anchor for the soul, firm and secure. It enters the inner sanctuary behind the curtain, where Jesus, who went before us, has entered on our behalf.*
>
> —Hebrews 6:19–20

You and I are no longer held in bondage without hope. Jesus has set us free! We no longer have to find a tabernacle or a temple in order to communicate with God. We no longer need to bring a lamb to the altar. Jesus has paid it all. We're saved by the blood of the Lamb.

> *When Christ came as high priest of the good things that are already here, he went through the greater and more perfect tabernacle that is not man-made, that is to say, not a part of this creation. He did not enter by means of the blood of goats and calves; but he entered the Most Holy Place once for all by his own blood, having obtained eternal redemption.*
>
> —Hebrews 9:11–12

Because Jesus sacrificed His life for you and me, we are redeemed. We have been bought up and paid off; we have been rescued, ransomed, and relieved of our burdens.

> *For Christ did not enter a man-made sanctuary that was only a copy of the true one; he entered heaven itself, now to appear for us in God's presence. Nor did he enter heaven to offer himself again and again, the way the high priest enters the Most Holy Place every year with blood that is not his own.... But now he has appeared once for all at the end of the ages to do away with sin by the sacrifice of himself.*
>
> —Hebrews 9:24–26

Jesus opened up the holy places for you and me to enter and stand in the presence of God, who has raised Jesus from the dead and set Him at His own right hand in the heavenly places (see Ephesians 1:20 and Mark 16:19).

As the Hebrew high priest brought the sins of the people to the mercy seat for God's forgiveness, we can come before the throne of grace and glory and God will show us mercy.

Consulting the Map

At the mercy seat, we see God showing His mercy to us. The dictionary defines *mercy* as "compassionate or kindly forbearance shown toward an offender, an enemy, or other person in one's power; compassion, pity, or benevolence."[1]

With that definition in mind, read the following verses and note how God's mercy is exhibited in each.

Exodus 34:6

_____

Numbers 14:18

_____

Deuteronomy 4:31

_____

Psalm 62:12

_____

Micah 7:18

_____

If we confess our sins, he is faithful and just to forgive us our sins, and to cleanse us from all unrighteousness (1 John 1:9, KJV). _Let us then approach the throne of grace with confidence, so that we may receive mercy and find grace to help us in our time of need_ (Hebrews 4:16).

As we come before the throne of grace for preservation and salvation, we can know that, just as the manna was given in the wilderness, so Jesus is our Bread and _provision_. As the Law was proclaimed by Moses, so Jesus sets down our _principles_ for living. As Aaron's rod spoke of God's authority, so Jesus, through His Spirit, gives _power_ to our personal ministries.

What an amazing book the Bible is! How perfectly the Word of God constructed the Old Testament, with the tabernacle, and brought it all together in the New Testament, with the Lord Jesus Christ. Could anyone but God have woven these plans and predictions into a such a beautiful garment, and then placed the mantle on you and me that we might stand in His presence?

> _And we, who with unveiled faces all reflect the Lord's glory, are being transformed into his likeness with ever-increasing glory, which comes from the Lord, who is the Spirit._
> —2 Corinthians 3:18

How exciting to know that as we come before our God with unveiled faces, we will reflect His glory. Although we've not been on the mountain with Moses or in the Most Holy Place bowing before the mercy seat, people will know we've seen the Lord because there will be a glow about us. As it was said of Joseph, Moses, and Daniel, those around them could tell that these men had been with God. According to Acts 4:13, people could see the difference when the disciples had been close to Christ: _When they saw the courage of Peter and John and realized that they were unschooled, ordinary men, they were astonished and they took note that these men had been with Jesus._

When we find God, others will notice the change! Not only will we look more radiant as we reflect the Lord's glory, but the Holy Spirit, the power and energy of the Trinity, will transform us into the likeness of Christ. Bit by bit, there will be changes as we commit our lives to Jesus and obey His will for us.

We will begin to manifest the fruit of the Spirit. As we stand in the presence of God, we will have more *love* for others than we ever thought was possible. We will be able to exhibit the *joy* of the Lord even in adverse circumstances. The *peace* that passes all understanding will keep our hearts and minds safe in Christ Jesus. *Patience* that we never had before will come over us in a wave of compassion and understanding. An attitude of relaxed *kindness* to others will replace our self-seeking nature, and a real *goodness,* a true desire to help, will become apparent to those we meet. For some of us who have wavered in our dedication to God in the past, the gift of *faithfulness* will be added, and people will see that we've been with Jesus. There will be a new *gentleness,* a softness in our face and in our actions that will attract people to us, and we will gain *self-control* over some of our habits and tempers that may have hindered others from seeking the Lord.

When we stand in the presence of God and bow before His mercy seat in repentance, He will forgive and transform us into new creatures in the image of His Son. And once we've seen Jesus — *the exact likeness of the unseen God* (Colossians 1:15, TLB) — we'll never be the same again.

Notes

Lesson 2

[1]*Barnes' Notes on the New Testament,* Bible Explorer Software, Epiphany Software, Inc., 2001.

Lesson 3

[1]*Easton's Illustrated Bible Dictionary,* Bible Explorer Software, Epiphany Software, Inc., 2001.

Lesson 4

[1]*International Standard Bible Dictionary,* Bible Explorer Software, Epiphany Software, Inc., 2001.

[2]Oswald Chambers, *My Utmost for His Highest* (New York: Dodd, Mead, & Company, 1935), 286.

Lesson 5

[1]Chambers, 45.

Lesson 6

[1]Rabbi Harold M. Schulweis, "Beware the Mere Mortal Who Guarantees Salvation," *Los Angeles Times,* December 17, 1978.

Lesson 7

[1]*Barclay's Daily Study Bible,* Bible Explorer Software, Epiphany Software, Inc., 2001.

[2]Elizabeth Dent, "Lord, Thank You for Being My Guide." Used by permission of the author.

Lesson 10

[1]Brother Lawrence, *The Practice of the Presence of God* (Old Tappan, NJ: Fleming H. Revell Co., 1958), 8.

[2]Ibid.

[3]Ibid., 52–53.

Lesson 11

[1]Chambers, 109.

[2]Ibid.

[3]Charles Spurgeon, *Morning and Evening,* September 18, Bible Explorer Software, Epiphany Software, Inc., 2001.

Lesson 12

[1]Chambers, 345.

[2]Poem quoted in an audio tape by Jack Taylor.

Lesson 13

[1]*International Standard Bible Encyclopedia,* Bible Explorer Software, Epiphany Software, Inc., 2001.

[2]*Random House Webster's Unabridged Dictionary,* "covetous."

Lesson 16

[1]*Life Application Study Bible* (Carol Stream, IL: Tyndale House, 1997).

[2]*Jamieson-Fausset-Brown Bible Commentary,* Bible Explorer Software, Epiphany Software, Inc., 2001.

[3]Kevin J. Conner, *The Tabernacle of Moses* (Portland: Conner Publications, 1974), 5.

Lesson 17

[1]*Easton's Illustrated Bible Dictionary,* Bible Explorer Software, Epiphany Software, 2001.

[2]Ibid.

[3]Chambers, 287, 344.

Lesson 18

[1]*International Standard Bible Encyclopedia,* Bible Explorer Software, Epiphany Software, Inc., 2001.

Lesson 19

[1]*International Standard Bible Encyclopedia,* Bible Explorer Software, Epiphany Software, Inc., 2001.

Lesson 20

[1]*Strong's Dictionary of the Hebrew Language,* Bible Explorer Software, Epiphany Software, Inc., 2001.

[2]*International Standard Bible Encyclopedia,* Bible Explorer Software, Epiphany Software, Inc., 2001, "relationships, family."

[3]Ibid., "shewbread."

[4]*Barnes' Notes on the New Testament,* Bible Explorer Software, Epiphany Software, Inc., 2001.

[5]Ibid.

Lesson 21

[1]*New Unger's Bible Dictionary,* Bible Explorer Software, Epiphany Software, Inc., 2001, "bless, blessing."

[2]Chambers, 348.

Lesson 22

[1]*Random House Webster's Unabridged Dictionary,* "mercy."

Personal Notes from the Journey

Personal Notes from the Journey

Personal Notes from the Journey

Personal Notes from the Journey

Personal Notes from the Journey

Personal Notes from the Journey

Real People... Real Life... Real Problems... Real Answers...
THE INDISPUTABLE POWER OF BIBLE STUDY

Through the Bible in One Year
Alan B. Stringfellow • ISBN 1-56322-014-8

God's Great & Precious Promises
Connie Witter • ISBN 1-56322-063-6

Preparing for Marriage God's Way
Wayne Mack • ISBN 1-56322-019-9

Becoming the Noble Woman
Anita Young • ISBN 1-56322-020-2

Women in the Bible — Examples To Live By
Sylvia Charles • ISBN 1-56322-021-0

Pathways to Spiritual Understanding
Richard Powers • ISBN 1-56322-023-7

Christian Discipleship
Steven Collins • ISBN 1-56322-022-9

Couples in the Bible — Examples To Live By
Sylvia Charles • ISBN 1-56322-062-8

Men in the Bible — Examples To Live By
Don Charles • ISBN 1-56322-067-9

7 Steps to Bible Skills
Dorothy Hellstern • ISBN 1-56322-029-6

Great Characters of the Bible
Alan B. Stringfellow • ISBN 1-56322-046-6

Great Truths of the Bible
Alan B. Stringfellow • ISBN 1-56322-047-4

The Trust
Steve Roll • ISBN 1-56322-075-X

Because of Jesus
Connie Witter • ISBN 1-56322-077-6

The Quest
Dorothy Hellstern • ISBN 1-56322-078-4

God's Solutions to Life's Problems
Wayne Mack & Joshua Mack • ISBN 1-56322-079-2

A Hard Choice
Dr. Jesús Cruz Correa • Dr. Doris Colón Santiago
ISBN 1-56322-080-6

11 Reasons Families Succeed
Richard & Rita Tate • ISBN 1-56322-081-4

The Fear Factor
Wayne Mack & Joshua Mack • ISBN 1-56322-082-2

Embracing Grace
Judy Baker • ISBN 1-56322-083-0

Courageous Faith
Keith Bower • ISBN 1-56322-085-7

5 Steps to Financial Freedom — Workbook
James D. Wise • ISBN 1-56322-084-9

5 Steps to Financial Freedom — Clothbound
James D. Wise • ISBN 1-56322-091-1

Forged in the Fire — Shaped by the Master
Tim Burns • ISBN 1-56322-086-5

7 Keys to Hearing God's Voice
Craig von Buseck • ISBN 1-56322-087-3

Balance at the Speed of Life — Workbook
Barb Folkerts • ISBN 1-56322-088-1

Balance at the Speed of Life — Clothbound
Barb Folkerts • ISBN 1-56322-092-X

Journey to Jesus
Florence Littauer with Marita Littauer • ISBN 1-56322-089-X